Illuminating Childhood

Also by Ellen Handler Spitz

Art and Psyche

Image and Insight

Museums of the Mind

Inside Picture Books

The Brightening Glance

Illuminating
Childhood

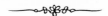

Portraits in
Fiction, Film, & Drama

Ellen Handler Spitz

The University of Michigan Press · *Ann Arbor*

Copyright © by the University of Michigan 2011
All rights reserved
Published in the United States of America by
The University of Michigan Press
Manufactured in the United States of America
⊗ Printed on acid-free paper

2014   2013   2012   2011   4   3   2   1

A CIP catalog record for this book is available from the British Library.

Library of Congress Cataloging-in-Publication Data

Spitz, Ellen Handler.
    Illuminating childhood : portraits in fiction, film, and drama /
Ellen Handler Spitz.
       p.   cm.
    Includes bibliographical references and index.
    ISBN 978-0-472-11754-3 (cloth : alk. paper)
       1. Children in literature.   2. Parent and child in literature.
3. Children in motion pictures.   I. Title.
PN56.5.C48S65   2011
809'.933523—dc22   2010030242

FOR

Abram, Michael, & Max

O children, next year, children, you will play
With only half your hearts; be wild today.

—ADRIENNE CECILE RICH

"Do any human beings ever realize life while
they live it?—every, every minute?"

—EMILY, FROM *OUR TOWN,*
BY THORNTON WILDER

Acknowledgments

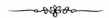

A great many people helped me as I wrote over the past several years, and my fear is that, inadvertently, I may fail to mention someone, an offense for which, should such an omission occur, I beg forgiveness.

First, my gratitude goes to the Erik H. Erikson Institute for Education and Research of the Austen Riggs Center in Stockbridge, Massachusetts, where, as Erikson Scholar-in-Residence during the autumn of 2008, in a picturesque setting replete with peacefully grazing cows and softly falling leaves, I made major uninterrupted progress on the manuscript. Among the exceptionally warm and friendly colleagues and staff, I should like to mention in particular Dr. M. Gerard Fromm, the Evelyn Stefansson Nef Director of the Institute; all my colleagues in (and beyond) the Greek tragedy seminar; and staff members Lee Watroba, Gary Harrington, Diane Tatro, Lisa Lewis, Jean Herrick, and Nadine Reddy, and librarian Robert DiFazio. Each member of that extraordinary community welcomed me.

Much of the writing was also done in France, and, among my Paris-based friends and colleagues, I wish to offer special appreciation to Marie-Thérèse and Alain Fabre, Rachel Rosenblum, and Annie Milgram. Filmmaker Alain Berliner accorded me an insightful morning interview at the Café Rostand, for which I am truly grateful. Among my Germany-based colleagues, I wish to thank Anke Lohmeyer of Kassel and Professors Berbeli Wanning and Jan Hollm; and, in India, Professor Diptirajan Pattanaik.

In Maryland, I received invaluable support from a variety of colleagues and others including Professors Gail Orgelfinger and Michele Osherow, as well as from Peggy Major, Beverly J. Conner, Perry Alexander, Avery Greene, and Daniel Gallaher. I want very much in addition to thank Cindy McLaughlin, John and Carol Geist, Annette Posner, Eleanor Wood, and both Kayte Pinter and Greg Hatem of Spoons Café in Federal Hill, Baltimore, who know just exactly how much dark roast coffee I need in the morning. My students deserve prominent mention, for they have brightened my days with their ardor and verve. An enormous debt of gratitude goes, sine qua non, to Dr. Thomas F. Lansdale III and Dr. Frank Ebert, whose medical expertise kept frail body from failing while mind cantered heedlessly on through the thicket.

Alison McKeen, now of Yale University Press, expressed faith in this unusual project from the start and helped me to find it this genial home. My deep appreciation goes unquestionably to Tom Dwyer, my editor at the University of Michigan Press, who supported me unstintingly, and to his worthy associate, Alexa Ducsay. I am grateful, at the Press, to other contributors to this project—Christina Milton, Heather Newman, and designer Heidi Hobde Dailey, and to the anonymous readers whose reviews helped me fine-tune the final version of the manuscript.

In the chapters called "Picturing Lost Children" and "The Mother-Artist," I have adapted material from my quarterly column "Apropos the Arts" in the journal *American Imago,* vols. 66, nos. 2 and 4 respectively, copyright, The Johns Hopkins University Press, 2009 and 2010. I hereby acknowledge the gracious permission of that press. Likewise, the chapter "Counting on You" draws on material from my essay "What Kind of Mother Are You?" in a volume called *Constructing and Deconstructing Women's Power,* edited by Beth J. Seelig et al., copyright, Karnac Press, London, 2002. Once again, my grateful acknowledgment is offered.

Writers work alone, and this book owes its being in the profoundest way to the indispensable friendship of Joanna and Peter Strauss (*primi inter pares*), to Jay Freyman, and to Sarah Lea Burns, Pradeep Dhillon,

Vivian Gornick, Mitchell Cohen, M. G. Lord, Florence Ladd, Eric Simonoff, Mary Ann Caws, Peter Jelavich, Lenore Malen, Yael Feldman, Mary Elizabeth Brewer Butler, Walter Marx, Maria Tatar, Susan Suleiman, Marina Warner, Ruth Alperson, and Derek Allen, many of whom have offered vital inspiration across oceans and continents.

To my far-flung family members—Vermont-, Massachusetts-, Virginia-, and Maryland-based, as well to those dear ones whose faces and voices live on only in memory, I note simply that they inhabit every sentence I write. For the sweetness of their affection and for their patience with me, for their wisdom, and above all for their love, I acknowledge them here.

Contents

A Welcome to My Reader

If the subject be curious and interesting, the book carries us,
in a manner, into company and unites the two greatest and
purest pleasures of human life—study and society.

—DAVID HUME

When we open a book for pleasure, a magic door swings ajar, and a genial host beckons us enter. We are strangers in an unfamiliar space—a mansion, a tenement, a high-rise apartment, or perhaps a boarding school—and as we step over the threshold by turning the first pages, we crane our necks to take in the decor, colors, textures, patterns, a whimsical detail or two. We, perhaps, might listen for music, while trying to imbibe the aromas of whatever culinary delights await us behind kitchen walls. The host introduces us to new faces, and we encounter voices heretofore unknown and fresh ideas, perhaps even the start of a new friendship. Or not. For books, like social occasions, can prove disappointing. When they do, I tell myself to leave. But I tend to stay. Out of courtesy, respect, and in hopes the evening may improve, which it frequently does. Then, when the visit winds down, and the good-byes are murmured, I sometimes close the covers in an elegiac mood, suffering my own version of that childhood wish to make the present last forever. My modest hope, as I welcome you into these pages, is that you will find intellectual companionship, a nourishing repast—both aesthetically and psychologically—and that you will deem your visit well spent.

Reading Art for Life, Slowly

> They talked about art in a merely sensuous way, dwelling on outside effects, instead of allowing themselves to learn what it has to teach.
>
> —ELIZABETH GASKELL

Every now and then a parent grasps what a child is experiencing. You reach out to catch the invisible ball that has been tossed your way. Even when your throwback misses, the exchange brings mutual pleasure. It strengthens bonds of recognition and trust. But what enables us, at such times, to read it right? To meet children in the fullness of their imaginative quests, hopes, or sudden outbursts of anxiety and mirth? For, as we know, the otherness of children often proves radically opaque. The ball simply drops. Whatever membrane it is that separates us from childhood, from the young people we know and love, and from the fading photographs of ourselves as children and our parents and grandparents, our brothers and sisters, it may be permeable but it is not transparent. Aspects of children's lives whisper of worlds we can no longer reach. *Through the looking glass. Over the rainbow. Second to the right and straight on to morning.* Yet we must try.

I propose we consider learning from what some might deem an unusual source, namely, the arts. Taking a key group of works in several media, principally from literature and film of the twentieth century, I seek to probe them for their multilayered insights into the realm of parent-child relations. The intuitive sensitivity that comes into play when parents and children are at a loss and cannot articulate their needs or communicate what is motivating them cannot be imparted intellectually. It cannot be taught by precept or theory. It may, however, be cultivated through mindful attentiveness, through careful observation, and, eventually, through creative emulation. These ways of learning have been privileged from time immemorial in the arts—mastering the steps to a new dance, say, or messily discovering the properties of wet clay. Works of art—films, novels, plays, sculptures, paintings, music—offer countless opportunities for experiential, observational, and imaginative learning. Whether optically or in our mind's eye, we are invited to observe in thrall and to participate vicariously as fictional characters gesture and interact.

Paying close attention to them, we notice how they meet or miss each other's subtle cues. And as we watch, we learn. In her classic *The Drama of the Gifted Child,* Alice Miller (1981) shows us how, in compliance with societal norms, we often fail in daily life to experience our own genuine feelings. We turn away from "jealousy, envy, anger, loneliness, impotence, anxiety" (9). Through the arts, however, we can safely and without risk permit ourselves to feel intensely what has not been permitted to us elsewhere.

After all, the arts can and do play a crucial role in our understanding of psychology. Ordinary people read novels, attend movies, watch television, go to the theater and the opera, and visit museums and art galleries not solely to be entertained but also to learn about each other and ourselves. We do this unselfconsciously and informally. The following pages *formalize this quest for psychological knowledge in the domain of the arts.* I start with the premise that a gifted writer, filmmaker, painter, or sculptor has the ability to teach us as much in one scene or vision as a therapist can in a session or a theorist in a treatise. We simply have to attend, to look and listen concentratedly so as to learn from works of art. Offering a set of readings, all on the theme of parents and children, this book demonstrates that process. With you my reader at my side, using an approach drawn from art and literary criticism, aesthetics, psychology, and everyday life, I share experiences of thematically linked works in literature and film, as well as painting, photography, and sculpture. And I beg sincerest pardon in advance for not mentioning other fine interpreters of the works included here, for these pages are not intended as a typical literary study but as a highly personal hybrid work.

Two strands flow along in parallel. Often they seem to merge and cross. These currents are, first, the close, careful reading of works of art and, second, the effort to glean insights from them about family relations. In some chapters the first stream seems more vital and ascendant while in others the second overtakes it. My aim is to accord priority to neither but to develop them in tandem and to swim along the crest of their waves, using my characteristic sidestroke and trying hard not to go under. Thus, these pages can be seen as an inseparable mingling of art and literary criticism with inquiries into childhood and parenthood. Characters are allowed to come to life when they seem to do so; I refuse to be embarrassed to accept them, from time to time, as real, for this is, after all, the way art works its magic.

Although astonishing strides have been made in the sciences and technology, we remain woefully stagnant in the realm of human relationships. The most fundamental of all of these is that between parents and children, for this one precedes and prefigures the rest. In religion, politics, education, and the arts, the parent-child relationship forms an ineluctable paradigm. To evolve, we should seek insight outside the usual designated jurisdictions and jump nimbly out of our clichéd niches. To that end, the following pages, devoted to practice rather than theory, exemplify in vivo readings of texts, films, and other works so as to bring psychology and art together in action. Each chapter melds disciplinary perspectives too often kept separate: aesthetic attention, ethical inquiry, clinical observation, and private experience. Nourishing one another here, they fashion a set of hybrid readings that seek to illuminate our central theme.

Within and beyond the university, studies of human relations are handed over to the social sciences. The arts and literature are not officially deemed primary sources of knowledge about human motivation and behavior. Yet they should be. To situate the present endeavor in intellectual history, we can recall long-standing Western cultural traditions of interpretation that have treated the arts as primary sources of pleasurable knowledge (*docere et delectare, plaire et instruire*). An overview of ancient authors and thinkers—Aesop and Plato, for example, as well as Cicero, Virgil, and Horace—reveals that primary knowledge gained from the arts was construed as moral rather than psychological in nature or, since the notion of psychology itself is of modern vintage, as the knowledge of right action rather than the *understanding* of action independent of any moral assignment. Recently, however, a work by the philosopher Denis Dutton (2009) combines aesthetics with evolutionary biology to argue for uses of fiction that tally with my readings here. Dutton holds that stories, for example, serve (and have long served) adaptive purposes and fostered human survival by enabling us to experiment with a variety of surrogate scenarios without fear of reprisal. The arts allow us to read and explore the contents of other minds and to engage in thought experiments that involve problems, values, and meaning in our relations with one another and ourselves. The arts are thus a proving ground for life.

In our time, with the exception of books, films, and other art designed for the edification of children and of the genre of ideological, polemical, and political work made with a clear rhetorical thrust, the notion of linking art with instruction has fallen out of favor. Books concerning parent-child relations rarely mention the arts as vehicles for psychological knowledge. The shift away from art as a respectable site for teaching and learning—away, that is, from ancient rubrics—came about gradually, culminating in the late nineteenth century and its fin de siècle infatuation with the notion of art for art's sake. Modernism, with its emphasis on form, became a factor, as well as the doubt and nausea occasioned by devastating twentieth-century politics and catastrophic wars and genocide, which bored deep chasms between expression and edification. Modernism and postmodernism furthered and exaggerated these trends by shunning all conceptions of art that purported to purvey knowledge beyond their own insular media.

In arguing here for the value of seeking psychological truths, specifically about parents and children, in the realms of art and literature, I am thus espousing a position that rebels against contemporary inclinations but claims ancient roots. It is my belief that to use the arts and literature as avenues toward the understanding of other human beings and ourselves, both within and beyond our changing family structures, is not only to take advantage of a rich vein of pleasurable knowledge; it is also to behold art itself through powerful underutilized lenses. It is, moreover, implicitly to encourage the production of, as well as attention to, work that engages focally the vicissitudes of human emotion.

Much in the canon of the social science literature about parent-child relations tends to identify and label problems, propose solutions, exhort and admonish readers, present statistical and empirical "proofs," and advance specific recommendations. Some works devote themselves in addition to historical or theoretical argumentation. My approach here is devoid of any wish to give counsel. By focusing on a *living out of experience via the arts,* these pages present works of art as venues for exploration, milieus wherein parent-child dilemmas spring to life and can be unhurriedly pondered.

It might be worthwhile, furthermore, to say that, although each of the following chapters touches on themes central to an understanding of children and parents, several are devoted to themes rarely touched on in the prevalent literature. These include the question of why one becomes a biological parent and brings a child into the world at all and why that is rarely posed as such rather than taken for granted, the theme of the disempowerment of both children and parents toward one another and the world at large, the subject of cross-gender longings in children and of any identifications that challenge societal norms, the choices that parents must make between private and public responsibilities, the long-term fallout from parental secrecy, the themes of prevarication and hypocrisy and their uses as means of self-definition and separation, and the disjunction between love and understanding. Are gaps and conflicts between the generations inevitable? How valuable are verbal modes of expression versus gesture, touch, imagery, objectification, and reenactment? Isn't it fascinating that, whereas we locate the notion of conflict at the center of works of art and admire it there, we try so hard in life itself to tamp it down?

The chapters are grouped thematically. After a preliminary meditation on the experience of pregnancy as evoked by a quattrocento Tuscan fresco by Piero della Francesca, the first four chapters are devoted to works about young children and their parents in situations that foreground themes of mourning, gender, and exile. The next three chapters treat several sets of mother-daughter pairs notably embedded in societies that skew and twist their bonds. The final chapters address adolescence, adult children, and the theme of alienation in several forms. My purpose is to take up a series of dilemmas that may arise for parents and children as the young pass from birth and early childhood through the school years and puberty to adolescence and the early stages of adulthood. The works are international in scope.

First, I ask what happens psychically to a small child when one parent dies suddenly and the surviving parent must manage his or her own grief while continuing to perform the ongoing parental role solo. Jacques Doillon's 1996 film *Ponette* offers an exquisitely realized vision that lets us observe details such as the inventive scenarios concocted by a bereaved four year old in order to enact her split consciousness of death. She can pronounce words that mean her mother has died, but she cannot believe her mother will never come back. The film portrays this child's refusal to accept finality and her heroic attempts to lure and summon back her parent from the grave. We follow the young father as he deals ineptly with his daughter's apparent madness in the wake of his own bereavement. He is shown struggling to hold fast to their shattered life while not abandoning his daughter emotionally. Through delicately wrought scenes and the use of music, the film exposes ways in which parent and child, separately and together, try to live on in the face of mutual devastating loss.

Next comes a chapter that studies a young child who attempts to enact his cross-gender fantasies in an unyielding, uncomprehending world. *Ma vie en rose* (My Life in Pink), a 1997 film by Alain Berliner, portrays a seven-year-old boy who believes he is a girl. His belief makes ever-widening ripples that engulf his bewildered family, his neighbor-

hood, and his school. No one around him can fathom the persevera-
tive identification, but we are taken inside his vivid rose-colored daydreams and witness his brave attempts to evade the role assigned him
by the social order. Image after image draws us close, and we experience firsthand the potency of a child's desire, its stamina, its defiance,
and its challenge to the demands of a world outside.

As prelude to the next chapter, we visit an exhibition of photographs in Paris in order to consider what happens when parents who
love their children fail—for reasons beyond their control—to protect
them from harm.

Toxic secrecy forms the theme of the following chapter, which features a little boy whose parents cannot talk with him about events that
occurred just before his birth and during his infancy. When do concealments become dangerous for children and how do children intuit
and cope with them? *Mendel*, a 1997 film by Alexander Rosler, set in
Norway after World War II, probes this question. It traces the far-reaching effects of family secrets. If a child defies his parents, breaks rules,
and puts himself into situations of danger in order to find out what
happened in the past, must we not ask ourselves whether protecting
him from it—no matter how horrifying it is—may be more destructive
than revealing it to him in some way? Parents who have endured
trauma themselves, however, may be incapable of such revelation, and
this is a factor that cannot be willed. What then?

Savage rupture in a mother-daughter dyad at puberty comes next.
This is observed through the vibrant imagery of Jamaica Kincaid's
1985 novel *Annie John*. Kincaid recounts the story of a young girl growing up on the Caribbean island of Antigua, and we witness the death of
her idyllic childhood. Eventually we see her emerge as an ambivalent
and wary young woman. We learn how what cannot be directly expressed between two people assumes strange new forms in visions,
dreams, and transitory liaisons, as well as in physical symptoms and
withdrawal. Watching with the girl's eyes as she catapults from intimacy
into estrangement from her mother, we marvel at Kincaid's unsparing
revelation of the fierceness of this couple's struggles through false-

hood, betrayal, and alienation toward a mutual goal of uneasy separation. Vivid recurrent metaphors encode sequences in their intricate dance: one sensitive child tangling with her formidable parent.

Next we move through personal reminiscence to a brief reflection on how an artist's sense of dissonance between her private and public selves illuminates the way parents delimit their children's lives and mold them like clay with both salubrious and deleterious results.

Conflict between duty to one's country and duty to one's family comes next. How do parents' moral choices impact their children's lives? *A World Apart,* a 1988 film by Shawn Slovo, daughter of the murdered South African journalist Ruth First and Joe Slovo, who battled apartheid, is a fictionalized account of the script writer and her mother. She, the eldest daughter, entering adolescence, craves attention. She cannot fathom her parents' unavailability, which seems neglectful and cruel. Unfolding against the brutal epoch in South African history when the Bantu people were segregated, disenfranchised, and murdered, this chapter details the plights of three mothers and daughters in that fractured, chaotic time.

Three generations interact next in a setting awash with American racism and potential violence. Lorraine Hansberry's 1959 now classic drama, *A Raisin in the Sun,* paints a trenchant portrait of adult children who long for what their surviving parent can neither comprehend nor give. We meet family members who find themselves at cross-purposes not only on account of their personalities and predilections but also as a result of external forces that propel them in dramatically different directions. While love never fails, sympathy and identifications wax and wane across the divides of gender and generation. We are made to wonder whether parental love must inevitably feel coercive and ask what we really mean when we say the hurtful and accusatory words "You don't understand."

Finally, the penultimate chapter asks what happens when a child is born who seems a misfit and when all attempts to love and understand him fail. Doris Lessing's 1988 novel *The Fifth Child* explores how the birth of a strangely aggressive troll-like child called Ben alters the dynamics of his milieu. Lessing challenges myths about the sanctity of childbirth; she traces parental attitudes, cultural imagery, and persistent ideals that cast long shadows which shape the destiny of families.

Aristotle, as is well known, speaks in his *Poetics* of the catharsis of pity and fear. It may be that if we can confront emotions such as these in art and literature, as the ancient philosopher implicitly counsels us, we will be better equipped to grapple more gracefully with them when they erupt into our real lives, and vice versa, for we bring our selves and our histories with us whenever we visit works of art.

As a special critical tool for what follows, I wish to borrow—from the Russian literary theorist Viktor Shklovsky—the fruitful notion of "defamiliarization." This term refers to the idea that art often renders ordinary life uncanny and transforms the banal into the exceptional. By means of exaggeration and recontextualization, art estranges gestures, acts, events, and locations. Showing them to us at oblique angles, it creates new forms that disorient us and make us pay attention. Lifting us out of our perceptual lethargy, art refuses to let us blink.

Astonished, delighted, or dismayed, we find ourselves baffled by aspects of what we had previously taken for granted. Balancing precariously, we stand amazed as apparent truths dangle before us, spin, and flip over so as to bare aspects previously concealed. At times art may even present us with atrocities disguised in shimmering mantles that inveigle us so that we feel tempted by their momentary allure whereas in reality they would give us only pain. By means of such acts of defamiliarization, art alters our gaze. Images and scenes parade before us expanding, contracting, reversing, unraveling, and pressing on to their utmost limits. To engage with them with our spines (as Vladimir Nabokov once put it) is to absorb what daily life rarely grants. It is to wonder and wander psychically, as when we were children, and to reimagine what is not.

As you read through the following pages, which need not be done in any special order despite the loose-fitting overall design, you may experience a slower-paced reflection in the presence of works of art than you are accustomed to in an age when the rapid amassing of uninterpreted facts has gained sway. Speedy, data-driven information gathering, moreover, is peculiar not only to the Internet and other electronic media; it is also the modus operandi reflected in voluminous shelves of how-to manuals and in the cultural literacy canon, where parents (and children) are cajoled and cautioned as to what they should and should not read. Here, by way of contrast, I have taken the liberty of moving slowly and drawing your attention to a number of lesser-known works of art rather than staying within the canon. I am pretending that, having entered, you are now traveling with me, like Dorothy and her friends, sharing full measures of radiant color, sudden anxiety, glittering hope, and ever-present adventure so that when we return to the flatter, grayer lands from which many of us come those landscapes will appear to have been—at least slightly—transformed.

Great with Child

Lorsque l'enfant paraît, le cercle de famille
Applaudit à grands cris. Son doux regard qui brille
Fait briller tous les yeux . . .
                              —VICTOR HUGO

When the baby appears, the family claps with joy. Her
sweetness glows and brightens the eyes of all who look
upon her. (My free translation)

Before the birth of children, fantasies may effloresce in the psyches of pregnant women and their partners. Thus, before there is a real baby there is an imaginary baby, an inner mental infant who occupies space in a woman's mind just as the fetus shares her body. Men, it is very important to say, have such fantasies too. What is it like to be in that mental as well as physical state? To be expectant or, as another saying goes, to be *with child?* To be carrying within you a being soon to be born? An unknown being, for whom you will have responsibility and concern for as long as you and he or she survive? As one colleague (an Amsterdam-based art historian) said to me gravely, "The moment I gave birth to my first child, I realized I would never again be free from worry." An extreme statement, perhaps, but not abnormally so. What can we learn about this state when we turn to the arts?

Most of the works of art to be met with in these pages are of modern

Piero della Francesca (ca. 1432), *Madonna del Parto.*
(Courtesy of Art Resource.)

vintage—movies, novels, a play—but I have chosen to open this exploration of art's wisdom with an image painted over five hundred years ago. Frescoed on the wall of a parish church in Tuscany, this glorious but insufficiently well-known masterpiece by the enigmatic Italian Renaissance painter Piero della Francesca was made, according to Giorgio Vasari's sixteenth-century *Lives of the Artists,* when the celebrated master returned from Rome to his mother's and his own birthplace of Borgo San Sepolchro on the occasion of her death. Vasari's brief mention of the painting can only strike a reader who knows the picture as uncanny for, although he describes its two large angels as very beautiful, he fails to pen a single word about its principal subject, namely, the statuesque figure who stands between those two angels and who lends her name to the picture—the figure on whom we are meant to focus, the figure whom the angels are presenting to us. It is none other than the *Madonna of Childbirth,* the pregnant Madonna, the *Madonna del Parto.*

Vasari, whose account has long been discredited by scholars for its mythic and elliptical albeit embroidered qualities (Piero had died decades before Vasari was born), possesses nonetheless some narratively evocative overtones, and we must read him in the lacuna made by a dearth of contemporary sources. Vasari tells us that Piero was called "della Francesca" after his mother because she was still pregnant with him when his father died and because it was she who brought him up, nurtured him, encouraged him, and supported all his artistic and mathematical pursuits. Even if only partly true, that story adds both resonance and pathos to what may be the most contemplative image ever made in all of Western art on the subject of expectant motherhood.

I want to hazard a performative account of this painting and take you with me to see it as I beheld it before it was removed in 1992 from its original site to the wall of a local museum where it can no longer fully accomplish its transcendent magic. For in its own village church in the middle of the little cemetery of the Commune di Monterchi, pregnant women had come to it for centuries, flocking to pray at its feet. They came asking the Madonna to grant them safe childbirth and an easy delivery. Art—as the noted Soviet film director Andrei Tarkovsky

(1991) and many others have said—belongs to the place where it is first created. Indeed, the very removal of Piero's fresco from its home inspired Tarkovsky to go to Italy, where he shot many complex images of the *Madonna del Parto* for his 1983 film *Nostalghia*. Tarkovsky's diaries from the period report that when the local authorities announced that the fresco would be taken away (presumably for conservation purposes) and put it into another building local women protested bitterly and pleaded for its continued presence among them. They begged that it be allowed to stay. Their fervent appeals were denied.

Imagine climbing, on a hot summer morning, a hill in Tuscany. The weathered gravestones lie strewn around us. We enter the small chapel that once contained the *Madonna del Parto*. In the gloom, a large image appears—a pensive young woman robed in iridescent blue flanked by two angels. It is she, Piero della Francesca's *Madonna of Childbirth*.

The moment I beheld her, time and circumstance were swept away. Nothing I had seen before captured the uncanny quality of pregnancy as did this painting. Restless waiting. That sense of hovering on the precipice of destiny. Inhabiting an alien time-space. Being utterly alone while joined to an as yet unknown being. Feeling supremely important while at the same time utterly insignificant, a mere vehicle, about to be changed irrevocably, separated forever from one's former body-self, suspended in a no man's land, knowing that one momentous, uncontrollable rupture is about to occur in one's body despite one's will one knows not when. Alone in the chapel, I stared at the painting until finally, faint and spent, I emerged into the sunlight. Did anyone else in the world, I remember wondering, feel this way after seeing this picture? And if so, how would I ever know? For, after all, to experience such beauty is not necessarily to be able to speak about it. Used as we are to explaining things, we are often at a loss for words in the presence of a work of art, which simply *is*.

Later, in Cambridge, someone read a poem. As I listened, sensations of that Tuscan scene rushed back with all its heat and fatigue, its amazement, faint nausea, and vertigo. The poem, by Jorie Graham (1983), is called "San Sepolcro," and it brought back the pregnant Madonna's blue dress and her abstracted gaze, her delicate, quivering fingers as they hover over the buttons on her bulging belly and the angels' wings; my earlier sensations flooded back into consciousness. And, although the beauty was of a different kind in this second incarnation, it was both palpable and real. Reflecting on these two moments, I am struck by their demand for complete absorption. Absorption, moreover, which is a state that pregnancy itself requires, a turning away from the world. This is a notion that was once remarked on by D. W. Winnicott (1956), the British pediatrician and psychoanalyst, who felicitously named it "primary maternal preoccupation." Women who are with child, he noted, exhibit tendencies to withdraw deep within themselves and to allow the external world—if they can—to fall away.

The notion parallels exactly what happens when we are caught up in the intense contemplation of a work of art or literature. It recalls, in fact, an often overlooked moment in Sigmund Freud's (1905) famous "Dora case" when he reports that his susceptible young patient "went alone to the painting gallery in Dresden, and stopped in front of the pictures that appealed to her. She remained two hours in front of the Sistine Madonna, rapt in silent admiration." The learned doctor goes on:

"When I asked her what had pleased her so much about the picture she could find no clear answer to make. At last she said, 'The Madonna.'"

Puzzled by these words, Freud failed to grasp the import of the girl's diffident and laconic rejoinder. We, however, may feel a rush of warmth for Dora and comprehend exactly how, enthralled before a work of art in all its wonder and presence, she could find no account to offer, no verbal equivalent for what she saw. We speak, after all, of such moments themselves as *pregnant*. And William Butler Yeats (1928), in a poem called "Among School Children" that refers explicitly to pregnancy, makes a related observation when he write that "both nuns and mothers worship images."

Like a live human body, Piero della Francesca's *Madonna del Parto* possesses a corporeality of its own and even a species of mortality. With boundaries and recalcitrance, it occupies, commands, and demands space. That morning in Tuscany it stood before me in my line of vision and greeted and arrested me. If I had failed to notice it, it would have objected. Ob*ject*ed. To accent the second syllable pushes the thought along (from the Latin *obiicere,* "to throw against"), to protest, refuse, put up a fight. Say no. The work of art in this dynamic behaves almost like a child in the first throes of negation, separation, and differentiation. The painting emerges out of its background, its tradition, its matrix. As in a birth. It detaches itself from the wall; it comes forth.

And the Madonna asks to be dealt with gently. She wants to be recognized, registered, and acknowledged. Not necessarily understood. We, too, ask something from a painting. Perhaps, on both sides, it has to do with love. The painting slowly and tenderly enwraps us in its folds of cerulean; it proffers an embrace. Then, as our eyes range over its surfaces, it pushes us away. Rejects us and withdraws into a realm of its own. Yet again, lush and ornamental, it lures us back into that golden curtained space. Once again we find ourselves inside a dome where buttons are coming undone and momentous events are about to occur. Bewitched, like the young girl herself, we find ourselves in a parallel trance.

The pregnant Madonna refuses to let go. To return her gaze, to attract her gaze when she withdraws and refuses us, we must move in close.

"Look at me," she says. But then,

"I don't care."

So we move away. Back and forth. In this way, we can get to know her. We discover nuances, secrets—the green and red and then the red and green of those twin angels' wings, the rhythms of their counterpoint. Shifting, circling, adjusting the stance between ourselves and the image, we find that it slowly dissolves so that its surface melts before our eyes and it quite transforms into a mirror. Familiar now, the painted surface begins to reflect us to ourselves—like a friend, a double, a twin. Reminding us of our own pregnancies or the pregnancies of those we love, it entwines us in gossamer threads of fantasy so that protracted daydreams appear to us along with half-remembered hopes and fears, forebodings, yearnings, the myths of our mutual existence.

And we feel a pang of responsibility for all this beauty. For the blue and the gold, for the richness of the drapery and the girl's distracted face and the buttons coming open. For the skin and bones and body. The painting's crust, its texture, its faint odor perhaps. And the dust. The web of cracks that waffle its face. Did they come much later? Or shall we imagine them like little birthmarks? Those extra lines. Traces of false starts, perhaps, in some long past process of creation, residue of moments when Piero's hand and brush may have trembled or when his mind lost and regained its concentration. Or are they the scars of afterpains? Perhaps they are birthing marks that betray the traces of an eruption. How did it happen, anyway, this painting? Fast? Or did it come slowly? With anguish? With joy? Was it a good labor or did this object make its entry agonized and protracted into the world that was awaiting it? And what kind of a world was that? A world, I suspect, that may not have been quite ready and did not hold out its arms in ardent expectation. Someone may have cheered or cried or just relaxed and sighed. Or perhaps the actual moment itself was anticlimactic and Piero simply kept wondering whether he had actually finished the painting after all and whether it had crystallized his dreams. Or what his mother might have thought of it (for no one would ever love him again, after her death, as much as she).

However vibrant it appears, the painting cannot live forever. Even in a holy chapel. Or in a museum, where it is given clean air to breathe and its temperature controlled and where it is protected from excessive moisture and light and provided with round-the-clock guards to protect it from harm. Still, it can be hurt. Bombs explode. Slashers break in. It is only composed, like us, of perishable matter. Sharing space with it, therefore, is to feel a special empathy and pity for it. An intimate knowing, a fleshly knowing with a bond akin to touch. For the work of art is a bit like a person. Even a religious icon, which teaches us that worth comes from cherishing. And, just like beings in the world of earth and plants and animals, it deserves participation in an ethos of care. An ethos undermined in a culture that is debased with debris from neglected and abandoned objects. Unmothered. Stillborn.

To share life space with a work of art—with a novel, a film, or a painting (for two hours, perhaps, like Dora in Dresden)—may be to enter into a unique closeness that shuts out the world. As in the

Madonna del Parto's preoccupation with herself and what is happening to and inside her body and soul. One may feel proprietary and protective. Exclusive, entitled. One may want to keep all to oneself, private and solitary, or one may burst with desire to share what is happening, although that can prove difficult, or to give birth to something utterly new out of gratitude, as a response to the experience—as perhaps I have tried to do in this small book—something that radiates multidirectional beams: bonding with the past, illuminating the present, gliding into the future.

When a Parent Dies

She told me to learn to be happy.
—JACQUES DOILLON

By adulthood, most people have developed some viable strategies for protecting themselves from being overwhelmed by grief at times of bereavement. Yet how do we prepare children and comfort them when final loss occurs? How can we better understand their experiences so as to be able to interact more sensitively with them when death comes close? How can we succor and support them, intercede for them, interpret to them, shelter them from excessive pain? Addressed by many eminent writers in the mental health disciplines over a course of decades (see, preeminently, Wolfenstein 1966, 1969, 1973), these questions are posed graphically in a 1996 French film called *Ponette*. This film teaches us in ways that differ from psychological case studies and theoretical treatises. Written and directed by Jacques Doillon who, not coincidentally, was born in France during the Second World War, it stars an astonishingly gifted four-year-old child actress, Victoire Thivisol, who was honored for her performance with the Best Actress Award at the Venice Film Festival. Released by Les Films Alain Sarde Rhône-Alpes Cinéma, *Ponette* won the New York Film Critics Circle Award for the Best Foreign Film of its year and was subsequently made available in video and DVD formats with English subti-

Ponette (1996, France), directed by Jacques Doillon.
Shown: Victoire Thivisol. (Courtesy of Photofest.)

tles (Fox Lorber FLV 1371 VHS). In what follows, all the translations of spoken words are my own.

Recounting the story of a small girl who loses her mother suddenly in a car accident, the film offers luminous perspectives on childhood mourning. In so doing, it demonstrates the value of studying works of art for their psychological insight. By presenting a comprehensive and masterful portrayal of a small child's suffering and incredible resiliency in the face of final, devastating, incomprehensible loss, it also considers significant parenting issues that surround bereavement when the survivor is a young child, and it offers us opportunities to reflect and imagine alternatives.

Briefly, the film recounts a story that begins with the image of a little girl, Ponette, whose arm is in a cast. She is being taken by her father by car to visit an aunt and cousins in the country. It is clear that the aunt is her father's sister. Gradually, we come to learn that the child has been in an automobile accident. On the car trip with her father, she finds out that her mother, who had been driving the car when the little girl's arm was injured, has not recovered. Ponette's father tells her this and then, arranging for her to stay with her aunt and cousins in the country, he leaves her to go back to the city to work (and, presumably, to mourn alone). Thus, the child is deprived of both parents. We are given a glimpse, in a brief scene, of the funeral. We shadow Ponette at her aunt's home with her two young cousins. Finally, we see her at her cousins' school among other children. Her father returns several times for visits. During this time, Ponette shows that she can, on one level, both understand and repeat that her mother is dead but, on another level, she does not understand at all. What she cannot accept is the emotional reality of this deprivation, and she believes therefore that the loss can be reversed and magically undone. In her efforts to retrieve her absent mother, she demonstrates the powerful fantasy life of a young child under duress, particularly under circumstances of catastrophic loss.

Moving step by step through selected scenes from the film, I want to linger on those that seem especially fruitful for an inquiry into parent-child relations, and at each juncture I shall raise issues motivated by the action and the representational choices presented on the screen.

Let's think first about the music which, heard immediately when the film begins, plays a significant affective role. In *Ponette*, this role can be interpreted in many ways because musical sound appears to acquire special significance, in Western cultures, under circumstances when the loss of human life has been experienced. In some non-Western cultures music likewise plays an important role. In the rituals of mourning in India, for example, among Hindus, the singing that accompanies the ritual of the dead is often a loud chorus performed well after the mortal remains have been consigned to the flames and sung in order to facilitate the progress of the soul toward a higher and higher spiritual order (Professor Diptirajan Pattanaik, Banares Hindu University, 2008, personal communication).

Here the meaning of the music is amplified because the principal mourner is a small child whose capacity for verbalization about her inner life is limited. Music, then, is made to carry some of what might otherwise have been put into words. Because of the linguistic limitations of his four-year-old protagonist, then, and for aesthetic reasons, the director took—so it seems—the step of prominently featuring music by the composer Philippe Sarde, whom he commissioned for this purpose. Sarde, who wrote music scored principally for solo violin with occasional piano accompaniment, carries poignantly the affects that animate this child's psychic life, her moods, her sorrows, her yearnings, her loneliness. Soulfully and plaintively throughout the narrative, the violin and piano are heard, often at times when Ponette appears alone, her mental state untrammelled by well-meaning others who tend to bewilder and distract her. Soft music wafts into our consciousness when the director, I feel, wants to convey something to us about her mental state apart from whatever action is occurring nearby and to make us aware of the profound disjunction that exists between outside and inside, the music standing, as it were, for the latter. Wordlessly, the violin and/or piano convey the quality of her feelings. And my reason, in part, for making this point now and dwelling on it is my wish to emphasize the difference between inside and outside, a difference that becomes amplified during trauma and bereavement. Thus, music not only serves as an aesthetic device but performs key psychological work in the film. It keeps us sensible of an external-internal division—a division we tend, protectively, to ignore.

What we encounter initially onscreen is the close-up of a snugly sturdy little girl with bobbed, slightly dishevelled brown hair that frames her softly expressive face. Four-year-old Ponette is seen in profile sucking her thumb through a plaster cast that covers her entire left arm. She is with her youthful father, and the first words are spoken by him. He tells her that he is going to draw a dog on her cast because, as he explains a moment later, he doesn't like casts to remain all white. Before speaking, however, he strokes her hair as she, in pajamas, lies in what appears to be a hospital bed. Thus, we are given right at the outset some defining parameters of the circumstances of our story and of the father-daughter relationship that will be central to our understanding.

Why, we may ask, does the father not want his daughter's cast to remain all white? What bothers him about that? As we learn gradually, the answer to this question has to do with knowing and not knowing. An all-white cast discloses itself. It announces that it is just precisely what it seems to be and nothing else. It proclaims the stark truth of its essence. All white and undisguised, it tells us without doubt that beneath it some body part, some element of a human self, has been broken. To cover the cast with drawings and pictures, however, might help to conceal it a bit and even give it a slightly different valence. Ponette's father wants this very much. He wants to avoid the painful knowledge that his little girl has been hurt. Yet, interestingly, he does not say he wants to decorate her cast in order to make it prettier for *her*. Why not? The reason, we sense, is that, though an adult and a parent, he, at this moment, can think only and do only what he feels to be right for *himself*.

As the audience for the film, we do not yet know the extent of what has happened to him and the child. We do not yet know that his wife was injured in a car accident while driving with their child and that she is no longer alive. By attending closely, however, to the way he speaks to his daughter, by noticing both what he says and what he does not say, we can tell that this father is stricken and that, rather than playing his usual nurturing role, he has been pushed to a place where he can do only what makes him feel better. And his subsequent denials, necessary for self-preservation, will grow ever more blatant. His drawing on the cast is the first evidence of this self-protective behavior. I want to point out that the director has refused to idealize this young parent. He has portrayed him authentically. He has sensitively recognized that, in the first moments following the loss of a beloved spouse, the bereaved man or woman who is also a parent may be rendered temporarily incapable of *being* a parent.

Ponette's father is not ready or able to attend to his daughter's needs. Before doing that, he must feel and dress his own psychic wounds. In comprehending this, Jacques Doillon may recall to our minds the words of Shakespeare's noble character MacDuff who, when asked to take his wife's and sons' deaths like a man, replies that first he must feel them like a man. In that interim, however, when the surviving (and now sole caregiving) adult is not able to perform his parental role fully, the bereaved child is left emotionally orphaned, and it is this state of affairs that is depicted during much of the action of the film. And while widespread unrealistic expectations about self-sacrifice and hero-ism in the parental role may make us tend to judge the father's actions harshly, what we must do is keep judgment at bay in order to sympathize with his grief and shock as well as with Ponette's. Only later will he be able to move on to a more altruistic position. If we watch him carefully, we can note the tender way he strokes his daughter's hair and sense the love he has for her. Aggression, too, of course, plays its necessary part in any bereavement, for we cannot help being angry on some level when loss occurs, and for many people being (actively) angry is easier than being (passively) sad. Interestingly, the dog Ponette's father draws ab-sentmindedly on her cast resembles an ambiguously cartoonlike lion.

Next we hear the roar of a car motor and find father and daughter on the road, again very close up in another zoom-lens image. Ponette, in overalls now, her hair pulled back with a headband, asks whether they are going home, but her father replies that they are going to her Aunt Claire's house in the country. Her face expresses puzzlement. Her father has given her no reason for this anomalous plan. After as-certaining that her cousins Matthias and Delphine will be there, Ponette next asks her father whether there will be lions there. Replying that her little cousins are not lions, her father fails to observe any con-nection between the drawing he has just made for her and her ques-tion. She asks again. This time, playing along with her fantasy, he tells her that the dog he has just drawn on her cast will protect her! And here we have a delicate and fascinating psychological moment because what the father misses is precisely the metaphoric valence of her ques-tion. In other words, what frightens Ponette is precisely her father's need to keep something back from her, to deny and conceal some-thing. She senses this, although she does not know what it is, and she dreams up the image of the lion, which is exactly right. The lion-dog he has drawn on her cast is a symbol of the same denial and avoidance that prevent him from telling her that her mother has died.

Why are they going to Aunt Claire's house instead of home? Where is her mother? There are so many unasked and unanswered questions. As the symptom of her father's anxiety, the lion-dog he has drawn cannot be used by Ponette as a cure for her anxiety. What we perceive here in microcosm is another small clue as to the unavailability of Ponette's father, his remoteness—despite his well-meant intentions—from her (and his own) thought processes. We see how profoundly wrapped up he is in the prison of his shaken self.

As they drive through the mountains, Ponette, in a gesture of self-protection from the glare of the sun, shields her small face. The screened image functions in a premonitory way. What we see is someone who does not want to look at the light, someone, metaphorically, guarding herself from knowledge of what is to come. She tries to put her head out the window (to escape, to hide, to see more, to see less), but her father says, sharply:

"*Non.*"

Then he tells her—and, in so doing, shocks the film audience—that he has purposely *not* strapped her in with her seat belt just so that she can learn what it is to be careful. By way of explanation for this egregiously irresponsible behavior, he says he is not like her "stupid mother," who, he implies, was a reckless driver and caused the accident that we have by now surmised, although it has still not yet been named as such. He repeats his insults against Ponette's mother in a tone of rising anger.

Visibly confused, upset, and still using the present tense, the little girl defends her mother:

"She is not stupid."

Holding her beloved rag doll Yoyotte in her arms, Ponette objects:

"It [meaning the accident] was not her [Mother's] fault."

But, consumed by the first wave of his own shock, rage, and disbelief, her father continues to make invidious comparisons between himself and his wife. What could she have been thinking? She wasn't drunk. She knew the road. And then:

"Did you ever get hurt with me?" he asks Ponette rhetorically.

At this point, a sudden shift takes place. The little girl, her arm in the cast, replies:

"I am not hurt!" (*Je n'ai pas mal!*).

To maintain herself psychologically intact and protect her mother from his rage, she, too, resorts to denial. She imitates her father by contradicting him. She adopts precisely the defense mechanism he has been using. She protests that her arm is *not* broken. And still she has not yet been told what happened. Her father, as we have seen by observing his successive behaviors—his disavowal of her wound, his irresponsibility toward her safety, his anger toward his wife, and his disparaging comparisons—cannot bring himself to say the words aloud that would acknowledge the reality of death. To speak these words would, in a very real psychic sense, make them true. For, as we know, unless and until words are spoken out loud by one human being to another we are capable of going on for long periods of time in fantasy states, pretending that what they signify is still false.

Ponette's father stops the car, they climb out, and we see them framed by mountains against a sky of blue. He gently lifts her up on his shoulders and then asks if she is happy up there. She replies simply:

"*Oui.*"

Next, with the violin softly playing off camera, he shocks us once again by asking her, in a matter-of-fact way, to make him a promise that she will never die and to spit on the promise. Still unaware of what has happened to her mother and therefore at this point still more tied to reality than he is, Ponette gently protests by querying her father:

"Even when we get old?"

Rudely, he brushes that realistic consideration aside and demands the promise a second time. She gives it and spits from his shoulders and then, at his request, repeats it in a stronger voice so as to satisfy him that it is real (as though to say something ever more loudly were to make it true).

Thus, in these early moments of the film, what we are witnessing is a dramatic reversal of the parent-child roles. This parent has, momentarily, become a child himself, and he compels the real child beside him, his daughter, to imitate him and at the same time to reassure him. Only after having extracted the necessary promise from her that she will never leave him does he feel ready to take the next step. He caresses her and takes her down from his shoulders.

Setting her small body down—of all places—on the hood of his car, he speaks the dreaded words:

"*Ta maman est morte*" (Your mother is dead).

Ponette's face at this moment must be seen and will not yield to my powers of verbal description. Her father then asks, "Do you know what that means?" At this point, she turns quickly away from him (away from the terrible words he has just pronounced) and climbs farther up on the car to its roof. There, she turns around and says:

"*Oui.*"

And then, almost immediately, by way of explanation and elaboration and, of course, denial:

"She is flying with her magic mirror."

"She is *dead*," her father repeats in a firm voice.

Matter-of-factly, he describes to her his own experience of loss. Like a small boy, he, too, thought she would be with them forever. He always felt good when she was there. He always knew that he could be as silly as he wanted because he could trust in her good sense and her ability to take care of Ponette so that he would not have to worry. Thus, just at the moment of breaking the news to his small daughter that she has lost her mother he burdens her yet again with his own feelings. And now Ponette herself, we can see, is beginning to break down. This time it is she who asks to spit. Mimicking him, learning from him, she repeats his words back to him and says she wants to spit now so that *he* will not die, and he, too, spits into her hand. Then he asks for her reassurance:

"Do you think I will be able to raise you myself?"

She again says "*Oui*" and tries to comfort him.

"She was all broken," he tells Ponette. There was nothing they could do to fix her. Ponette moves closer to him and says she will console him. Father and daughter reach for one another and embrace tenderly. And Ponette, held by her father, begins to cry. The scene ends.

Throughout this opening of the film, then, what we have seen, what we have witnessed, is a delicately wrought portrayal of how sudden death impacts characters who now find themselves altered and chained by what has been visited on them. The former divide between the generations, the responsibility gap, gender differences, inequalities in knowledge and experience—all of this melts away before the implacability of death.

I think that one must tread softly here and reflect compassionately on the issues of parenting because, as I have said, at such times even the most devoted of parents cannot and perhaps should not be expected to shine in a role that normally demands a high degree of altruism. Rather, as here, a parent must be allowed to regress despite the initial burden this inevitably places on his or her offspring. In some religious traditions, apropos, it is unacceptable for adult sons and daughters to offer eulogies at their parents' funerals or for principal mourners to prepare their own meals during the mourning period; the bereaved, even when they are parents themselves, are fed by others in the family and the community. Also, by analogy, we may compare the cautionary words of flight attendants on aircraft who say that parents must secure their own oxygen masks before assisting their children.

Ponette's father, young and inexperienced himself, has been, in this film, permitted to express and endure the stages of his own bereavement. While we must, I would aver, observe him tolerantly and sympathetically, we need not applaud his behavior. Just by noticing what he does and does not do or say, we may be stimulated to imagine other possibilities. This matters, and it is a gift of the film. By showing us so clearly, so unashamedly, so fully what happens psychologically in one particular situation, the director empowers us to reimagine the scenario in other ways. My endeavor, rather than supplying such alternatives, except perhaps implicitly by means of what I have chosen to point out, is to prompt you, by means of what I am offering here, to come up with choices and visions other than those represented onscreen in this work. Some such choices may seem overly idealistic, perhaps, and even beyond the reach of actual human beings with our sundry limitations, but, nevertheless, they may be choices and ideals to strive for. By imagining them, we stand to greatly enrich the tasks of parenting and teaching and even of psychotherapy.

The next major mise-en-scène is the funeral of Ponette's mother. I want to interject here that what we are actually shown onscreen now, as earlier, is not the wider context of the event but only what is perceivable by means of zoom-lens focus. Like Doillon's choice of music, this cinematographic choice brings together the psychological and the aesthetic so that one reinforces the other. The effect of this directorial decision is to bring us in as close as possible to the mental state of the little girl who plays the title role. We move as near as we can to her without actually getting under her skin, although at times even that seems possible. Uncannily, the directing, composing, acting, scriptwriting, and cinematography collaborate to achieve an effect that enables us to imagine ourselves inside the child's world and privy to what she is enduring.

Ponette's young cousins surround her: Delphine, who is a few years older; and Matthias who appears to be about her age. Clutching her beloved rag doll, Yoyotte, she listens to these children as they give voice to their own confusions and superstitions about death. Matthias, for example, speculates that sometimes in hospitals people get shots but that it didn't work for Ponette's mommy and that therefore (he proclaims decisively) she will never come back. When Ponette quietly responds with the non sequitur that "Jesus will take her up there," Matthias resolutely shakes his head:

"*Non!*"

Delphine, the self-assured big sister, her hair pulled back in a ponytail, a red scarf arranged jauntily around her neck, managerially instructs Ponette to offer a present to her dead mother and to place it inside the coffin. She suggests that this offering should be the doll Yoyotte because that is what Ponette loves best. Little Ponette balks at this idea; piteously refusing, she holds on to her dolly for dear life. Horrified, we in the audience silently pray that she will not give up this precious doll, which so clearly symbolizes for her the maternal relations that have been wrenched away from her. The voice of Aunt Claire is now heard asking to have the coffin opened so that the children may place their gifts inside, and we watch as Delphine solemnly deposits a note on paper (she is old enough to write) and a toy robot.

After the ceremony (which, because the camera has been focusing almost exclusively on the children, we never see), Ponette announces that her mother will be able to come out later.

"*Non!*" replies Matthias contrarily. He adds, "Only *zombies* can come out." And besides, he continues sagely, they put a heavy cross on top of you that makes it impossible for anyone to come out. Dazed, confused, and bereft, Ponette stands by listlessly as she tries somehow to process such well-meant but unhelpful pronouncements through permeable veils of misery, incomprehension, and loneliness.

Later, on a nearby hillside in the grass with just one pale daisy visible near their feet, their coats back on after the funeral service, Ponette and Matthias have wandered off together. Sympathetically, the dark, curly-haired little fellow, who is slightly smaller than she, tells her authoritatively that if they have put a pillow inside her mother's coffin she will sleep a long time. Then, noticing her stricken face, he adds kindly, "Don't worry. She has one, and she will sleep." He kisses Ponette on her cheek, and she, clutching Yoyotte, who has been returned to her, sadly but hungrily returns his embraces. As the two children try tenderly to comfort one another on the hillside, we feel the little girl searching and yearning in Matthias's childish kisses for the caresses of her lost mother. We recognize also in this scene, on another level, just how intimately connected all subsequent acts of love and affection are with the earliest manifestations of these emotions in the dawning phases of human life.

One central aspect of these scenes that I wish to point out is the bewilderment of the other children in the face of death and the strategies they use to cover up and manage their own intrusive fears. Bravado and apparent certainty rank high. No problem for them that their stream of solemn sureties proves logically inconsistent. As we see repeatedly throughout the film whenever the children talk with one another, their ideas and phrases and sentences possess a discreteness unacceptable in adult parlance; no explanation needs to be congruous with the preceding one for it to have resonance and clout.

The cousins also, I aver, should be seen as unwitting prey to a species of what might be called a kind of manic triumph, for it is, after all, not *their* mother but *Ponette*'s mother who has disappeared forever. Thus, their occasional spitefulness. They can afford it. Yet, as they hover about Ponette, inundating her with their ceaseless efforts to comfort and explain, they do so both for her sake and for their own. Thoughtlessly, but also in search of their own answers to unanswerable mysteries, they repeat fragments of what they have gleaned from adults at one time or another. Unlike Ponette, who is far too overcome emotionally to be puzzled intellectually, their principal efforts are to try to make sense of what, in fact, makes no sense. But their chatter occurs in a zone far away from that in which Ponette herself exists at the moment. We sense that she is present only physically while mentally she drifts, conscious vaguely of the snatches of babble that waft into her orbit and out. When she responds to them as best she can, it is always brokenly.

The funeral is now over. Ponette's father can be seen at the wheel of his car ready to depart. He is leaving her behind with her aunt and cousins.

"Can I go back to Lyon?" he asks, seeking her permission to go and thus once again reversing their roles.

Promising that he will call her each night to hear about her doings with her cousins and about all their silliness, he switches the motor on.

Holding tightly to Yoyotte, Ponette lets out a terrible cry. He stops the car. Placing the burden of responsibility for *his* feelings yet again on *her* and at the same time prohibiting her from expressing *her* feelings—her sorrow, her regret, her loss—he threatens:

"If you cry, I will be sad all the way."

And then immediately he repeats, "I will start the car up again. Try not to cry this time."

But then, in an unexpected flash of inspired parenting, he does something quite wonderful: he initiates an exchange of tokens with her. After informing her that he will drive slowly so that nothing will happen to him, he suggests that, if she is scared, she should give him Yoyotte. In exchange, he says, he will offer her something, too, his favorite thing, his most prized possession—his watch. Unsurprisingly, Ponette, who had been unwilling to relinquish her beloved Yoyotte to her dead mother, proves equally unwilling to give the doll now to her living father, who, one feels, should probably *not* have asked for it. "I'll give you Teddy," she offers, and runs back to her cousins' house to fetch the stuffed animal and then passes it to him through the car window.

"Listen," her father tells her, "to the tic-toc," and he hands her his large-faced watch back through the window. "Listen to it when you are sad, and it will be like my heart beating." Ponette cocks her head and listens. "Teddy will take care of you," she offers, and he, pursuing their joint fantasy, agrees. "Yes," he concurs, "he will protect me."

As they kiss each other good-bye, we can see in the background of the frame in blurred focus an image of little Matthias held by the arms of his mother, Claire, who is squatting with him by the roadway observing the scene of departure. The juxtaposition of these couples—father with daughter and mother with son—appears both prophetic and symbolic. For, as the motor starts and the car drives away, we realize with a sinking heart that Ponette is now completely alone with no parents at all.

In analyzing the foregoing scenes, I want to start with the observation that the immediate abandonment of a bereaved child by her living parent deals an especially devastating blow and should, whenever possible, be avoided. Of course, in this case we must accept the terms of the film. We are made to understand that the father's return to Lyon for purposes of work precludes his taking Ponette with him and that he has thoughtfully worked out an alternative plan for her. It is clearly his hope that a stay in the country with her aunt and cousins will prove salutary and even pleasurable. Nevertheless, what this actually means to Ponette is that the loss of her mother is now compounded.

Why does she refuse to give up her doll? She cannot relinquish it either to her dead mother or to her living father. Of course, in an important way, the answer seems obvious: Ponette's emotional need for Yoyotte is palpable. We are instinctively shocked when Delphine commands her to throw Yoyotte into the coffin, and we almost want to cry out loud:

"No, don't! You mustn't."

But why? How does the doll function for Ponette? What makes Yoyotte so important? From a point of view based in psychology and psychoanalysis, it seems clear that this floppy plaything represents just those qualities and characteristics described by D. W. Winnicott (1953) in his classic article "Transitional Objects and Phenomena." Yoyotte seems to be for Ponette precisely the unique, highly invested "not-me" possession, the irreplaceable special object, which signifies and embodies elements of the relationship she has had with her now departed mother. How, under the circumstances, can she give it up?

A later scene bears out this interpretation. Ponette, who chooses to remain in her pajamas during the daytime after her father's departure, has been refusing to play with her cousins. She wants to be alone because she feels uncomfortable with the other children, who want to play normally and cannot understand what she is living through. Their lively presence feels intrusive to her. As we have seen, their behavior and words have also at times been cruel. Ponette tries to share her fantasies with them by telling them that her mother comes to her at night and plays with her. When they refuse to believe this, she counters:

"Ask Yoyotte."

This in turn brings taunts from Delphine and a disgusted retort that dolls cannot talk. Finally, after the two cousins leave in exasperation, Ponette picks up Yoyotte and says:

"*They* think you cannot talk."

Having been ridiculed by the departing Delphine and told sarcastically to "play with Yoyotte and your mother," Ponette begins to do so. Assuming the role of mother, she suddenly grows angry and "disciplines" Yoyotte for not tidying up her room. She throws the doll savagely on the floor, and in so doing she unconsciously replays the scene of the accident. Redoing its ending by making everything come out all right in her play, she picks Yoyotte up, hugs her, kisses her, and comforts her.

"Don't be scared," she tells the doll as if she were its mother, except that, of course, in life it was her mother who had the fatal accident. During this play, she repeats to Yoyotte what her father had told her:

"*Maman, elle était tout cassée*" (Mommy was all broken).

By uttering these words just at this juncture, she reveals the deeper significance of her game—the throwing of the doll and the comforting of it. And, in her fantasy here, the doll has taken on multiple roles—that of mother, confidante, alter ego, and child—and we can see how complex and variable its meanings are. Through the intensity of this layered play and its metamorphic richness, Ponette is able to relive and rework the trauma. In doing that, she reveals the symbolic valence of the toy within the parameters of her inner life. The phenomenon becomes clearer: the doll cannot be given up because it exists not only as a "thing" but as an integral part of the little girl's psychic life. At one point Ponette herself even indicates that she grasps the notion. She says quite plainly:

"Only I love Yoyotte."

What she clearly means is that she alone can love Yoyotte because in a very real sense Yoyotte qua Yoyotte exists only for her. To anyone else, the doll would count merely as a scruffy object.

A word, before we move on, about the exchange of tokens. This seems to me a rare instance of inspired parenting on the part of Ponette's beleaguered father. I am moved not only by his notion per se of the token as a viable substitute for absence but by his unquestioning acceptance of Ponette's immediate refusal to give up Yoyotte and her offer to substitute Teddy.

"Go get Teddy," he responds immediately without hesitation. It is as if, intuitively, he comprehends the admonition that we must never question the child's attachment to her special object for fear of breaking the spell and robbing it of its unique properties. I also very much like his offer of his watch because this seems to me an ideal token, not only because it symbolizes his beating heart, as he points out, but because it constitutes a tangible representation of the passage of time, and time is, after all, our most perceptible measure of separation. I like the way he tells Ponette that her aunt should make another hole in its strap so that she can wear it on her tiny wrist (this actually occurs) and also the fact that a watch is a sensually rich symbol that appeals at once to sight and touch and hearing. Even to smell, perhaps, if the band be leather, but that, of course, we have no way of knowing.

At any rate, an additional boon occurs when, after Ponette tells him that Teddy will look after him, he solemnly concurs. By doing so, he enters into her fantasy. They make a pact. Exchanging their mementos, they seal a bond. This has, I feel, significant and empowering consequences for Ponette, even though at the moment of its execution her sense of impending loss diminishes it and limits her capacity to benefit from it. The parting moment also, I want to suggest, signals to us, in the audience, that we have here a father who, once his own psychic wounds have begun to heal, will be capable of returning to his daughter and of reinvesting in her and in the joys of parenthood. The tokens are multiply determined; we may interpret them not only as pledges by father and daughter to remember one another during absence but also as signs of hope for the future, for reunion, and for good things, perhaps, one day, to come. This second pact, with its exchange of meaningful tokens, represents, therefore, a significant psychological advance over the earlier pact—the mutual spitting and promises never to die. The process of mourning is well under way.

In the following scenes, we discover what happens to Ponette when she is left behind by her father. I would like at this point to turn for a moment to the work of the New York psychologist Martha Wolfenstein, who was renowned in the 1960s and 1970s for her clinical work with bereaved children. Wolfenstein wrote eloquently of her young patients' tendencies toward what Freud called the "splitting of the ego," meaning that, while they were able verbally to acknowledge the death of their parent, they often could not, on a deeper level, accept this truth and denied it in manifestations of their fantasy life and daily behavior. Ponette seems to illustrate this theoretical principle. She dreams about her mother at night, and she fiercely holds on to and protects her mother's good image in her mind. Vehemently, she believes in her own power to alter the unwelcome reality and bring her treasured mother back to life. At one point, apropos of this point, her little cousin Matthias reminds her that their grandfather (Papy) has died, and he, too, was buried, and since then *he* has never come back. Ponette, however, is unfazed by this objection. Significantly, she counters:

"No one was waiting for him."

Thus, she implies that because *she* is waiting, because she cares, because she *needs* her mother, her mother, unlike Papy, will return to her. What we observe in her answer, I want to interpret, is, in part, the sturdy, stalwart egotism and self-confidence of a well-loved child.

Ponette takes to sitting on a hillside outside her aunt's house for long hours with Yoyotte and sometimes with other toys, simply waiting, waiting for her mother to come back. All the while, however, she is perfectly capable of acknowledging verbally that her mother is "dead." Thus, we can see this theoretical notion, the splitting of the ego, demonstrated and enacted before our eyes on the screen; we witness it *in statu nascendi.*

Claire, in a well-meaning effort to comfort her little niece, whose abnormal behavior over a period of several days is beginning to concern her, takes her in her arms one day and recounts to her the Christian story of how Jesus died, was placed inside the tomb, came out again later, was resurrected, and is now peacefully ensconced in heaven. This story is meant, of course, to reassure Ponette that her mother is perfectly happy now, too, and is with Jesus in heaven. Listening intently to her aunt, however, Ponette immediately wants to know whether *this* will happen also to her mother. Not quite understanding the force of *this* in Ponette's question, Claire says that, in fact, yes, it will happen to all of us.

"When?" The child wants instantly to know.

"When God wants it to happen," her aunt replies, tenderly stroking the little girl's hair. But, Ponette protests logically, "Mother wanted to stay with me! She did not want to go to heaven." And at this point, her aunt begins, with a glimmer, to realize that the story she had intended to be so helpful may in fact have proven more confusing and unhelpful to the child than she could have predicted. Later on, after days have gone by and Ponette has continued to wait for her mother to come out of her grave (as Jesus did) and has refused to eat and become increasing disconnected from the ongoing life around her, her aunt, understanding how difficult it has been for this four year old to process the story she told her, apologizes to her. But the apology can only fail as the initial story did. At this point, we are made sensible of how adults, with the best of intentions, often mistake the effect of their words on the minds of young children, who tend to hear them literally and in terms of specific circumscribed contexts of their own.

It is doubly awkward that Ponette's father directly and vehemently contradicts her Aunt Claire on these matters of religion. Called back to his sister's country house from Lyon because of the child's aberrant behavior, he appears without warning at the end of a poignant scene in which, once again, she has been waiting outdoors in the grass for hours for her mother to come out of the grave and return to her. We see her small form alone silhouetted against the evening sky, her back to us. She has tried conjuring her mother up with magic words (*Ta-li-ta-cum*) that were made up a few days before by her cousins in a game Delphine had invented, whereby, after pretending to be dead, she then would joyfully resurrect herself over and over again by reciting these syllables. Ponette sits alone holding a small offering of leaves and pinecones she has picked. By now, with the violin playing soulfully in the background, Ponette has begun to sob heartbreakingly, for, as always, there is no tangible response to her magical efforts to end her hopeless waiting.

Suddenly, her father—the wrong parent—appears. He has driven two hours to get here, he tells her. She replies that she has a small present and holds out the bouquet of leaves.

"It's nice," he says, "too bad it's not for me."

He asks if it is for her mother, and she says it is for him, too, and then turns and runs away from him. Pursuing and catching her, he asks in a stern tone:

"How long are you going to wait for your mother?"

Upset and trying very hard not to be angry with her for so many reasons—angry because she is causing trouble for him and inconvenience for his sister and her family, angry because she is acting out what he is trying so desperately hard to efface and put behind him, angry because he feels remorse and guilt, and angry, perhaps above all, because anger is so much easier to feel than grief, he accuses her:

"Are you crazy or what?"

Shaking her head, her lips trembling, Ponette fights back the tears.

"Yes," her father says, "You are crazy." (*Tu es malade.*)

Frightened and feeling as though she is about to suffer yet another felt bereavement from this accusing father, Ponette backs away from him, but he presses on. Taking her firmly by the hand, he leads her toward the house. The camera follows them from behind.

"God doesn't talk to the living," he tells her. "God is for the dead, not for us. Your mother wasn't scared to die, so spare her this Jesus and God stuff. Live in the world with me and your cousins," he tells her. For him, religion is a lie, and, as he says firmly, he does not want her to lie to herself: "Lying won't make the hurting stop."

"You don't have to yell at me," Ponette counters in a broken voice.

"Than stop acting crazy, okay?" he replies.

"Okay," she softly agrees (*D'accord*).

The emotional impact of this scene is harsh and spasmodic. Whereas earlier, as we noted, it was Ponette's father who struggled against the reality of his wife's death and the little girl who needed to know what had happened to her mother, these positions are now reversed, and it is he who wants to force her prematurely—for her own good, as he sees it, as well as for the sake of those around her—to come to terms with it. But Ponette is not ready. I want to point out, though, that, despite the incongruity between their mental states at this point and despite the severity of her father's tone and language, the two of them betray a mutual love and concern that trump these temporary negative moods. Partly, I want to suggest, the reason he does not understand what she feels is that he simply cannot afford emotionally to do so. This is an important point and one readily comprehensible to us the moment we make an effort to experience the situation from his viewpoint. Precisely because we as the audience are standing quintessentially outside the film (even though we are, of course, also very much drawn in), we can afford, as it were, to understand and sympathize with a variety of emotional positions and not be caught up in a parti pris. Hence, once again, the value of such a work as a vehicle for the learning and teaching of profound psychological lessons.

After Ponette's father leaves once again for Lyon, the next scenes of the film take place in a boarding school to which she is sent with her cousins and a group of other young children. Here, as previously, Ponette tries repeatedly to find some way to reconnect with her mother. As background for her efforts, we are shown, in a series of scenes replete with empathy, pathos, and humor, the confusions of young children over a variety of issues such as religion, sexuality, and divorce, as well as death.

Aurélie, a young teachers' assistant in the school, takes Ponette, at one point, into the chapel or "God's room," as the children call it. Ponette caresses a large carved wooden statue of Jesus that stands on display there and prays to him at night to allow her to speak to her mother again and hear her voice once more. Meanwhile, she has been told by others that there is a little Jewish girl in the school called Ada who has been endowed with special powers (presumably because she is Jewish and therefore, supposedly, an *enfant de Dieu*) and that, if she were to hearken to this child and obey her absolutely, she, Ponette, might herself become a "child of God" and thus be reunited with her mother. Bewildered by all the conflicting stories and prescriptions, Ponette hedges her bets and, animated by unwavering hope, follows both the apparent Catholic and Jewish prescriptions. While by day in the schoolyard she complies with a series of tasks and trials that Ada insists she must perform, at night when she is alone she talks with God imagined as the statue of Jesus in the chapel.

Trying to be as good as possible, Ponette precipitates her "bargains with fate," as Wolfenstein calls them, covert efforts to coerce the lost parent's return for purposes of reward. At the same time, she has not forgotten her father's words about the lies of religion and repeats them to the devout Aurélie. Quoting her father, Ponette chides Aurélie for telling her stories about Jesus and reiterates her father's remark that such stories will not make the pain go away.

"It's not nice," she protests, "to tell me such stories."

Yet, not long after this exchange, the camera gives us an exquisite image of her, close-up in profile, her little hands clasped in prayer, the lion-dog plainly visible on her cast, praying, telling God that He knows her mommy is dead because she is with Him in heaven and asking God please to tell her mommy to talk to her because, although she has tried, her mommy has never answered her. Thus, the chasm between logical and psychological reality.

Of all the scenes that occur with the other children in the school, two are vital. After undergoing a series of trials with Ada as her guide, Ponette is at last told that it remains for her only to prove her bravery. Delphine and Matthias lead her, blindfolded, down a path to an unknown destination, which, they warn her, will test her courage. It is scary, they say, and, moreover, it stinks. She will have to endure it, however, only for five minutes. What they do is to force her to climb into a garbage can, and, while doing so, they take away her father's precious watch so that they can time her while she is inside it.

Frightened and repulsed but determined to do anything it takes to get her mother back, Ponette allows Matthias to push her in. The cousins drop the lid on top of her. The image is both horrifying and stunning because, of course, what we see is not only a garbage can per se but, symbolically, a coffin. The other children run away and discuss whether they should stay nearby or disappear. But suddenly they hear sounds of sobbing and realize that Ponette is crying. They rush back to rescue her. "It's all right," they tell her, "You succeeded!" Tear-stricken, her small, blotchy face appears as they lift the lid, and, in trying to extricate her, they accidentally drop the heavy lid of the can on her fingers, thereby causing a fresh outburst of wailing. It is a scene that dramatizes both the desperate determination and longing of the title character and the tempered cruelty of her peers. She will stop at nothing to achieve her goal of reaching her mother, and the other children, both comprehending and uncomprehending, seek at once to abet, assist, and thwart her.

Finally, a pivotal moment comes on the playground when a blond boy named Antoine enters with a toy gun. In this scene, a key fantasy about the fatal accident is enacted.

"Who wants to kill me?" Antoine challenges the other children as he brandishes his weapon. He goes up to Ponette and offers it to her.

"You can kill me," he dares her.

"I don't want to," she replies.

But he pressures her until, reluctantly, she takes the gun from him and complies.

"I'll shoot you in the head," she says, and pretends to do so.

He cries out in agony, falls to the ground, and then lies there on his back. Ponette steps on him at that point and then runs off with his gun. Antoine, furious at her now for having exceeded the terms of the offer and game he had proposed, chases her and tries to wrest the gun away

41

from her. She holds on to it fiercely and will not let go. Exasperated, he tells her that she cannot kill anyone else with it because it is *his* gun. Then, when she continues to refuse to give it up, he hits her, and they scuffle with one another. At this point, Antoine, in rage and frustration, pronounces words that articulate perhaps the most deeply buried level of her fantasy.

"You killed your mother!" he accuses. Relentlessly, he continues:

"She died because you were mean. When someone's mommy dies, it is because they were mean. My mommy isn't dead because I am not mean."

Shocked by these damning sentences, Ponette cannot maintain herself intact any longer and completely breaks down. With tears smarting in her eyes, she stands alone on the playground.

"If my mommy were here," she cries, "You never would have said that."

Shortly afterward, she tells her cousin Matthias that she wants to die.

In pondering this exchange, the central question that comes to mind has to do with the meaning of the gun and the killing to Ponette. Up to this time, she has expressed sorrow and grief and longing and determination and resourcefulness but never aggression. And yet, as we know, there is anger, too, when a parent dies. Anger, because the child, endowing the parent with superhuman powers, fantasizes that if a parent disappears that parent must, on some level, have wanted to leave or have chosen to leave or, perhaps, could have prevented the leaving. Even Ponette's father, as we saw, became angry and questioned why his wife had died in the car crash by imagining that the result was in her hands, as he asked:

"What was she thinking?"

Later, on in these pages, in the chapter "Counting on You," when we discuss the film *A World Apart,* we shall see how similar feelings arise in a young girl called Molly as her mother is dragged off helplessly to jail by the South African police.

Ponette, having been given a gun and asked to perform the act of "shooting" at the other child, gains, in so doing, the power to experience a certain kind of relief. She is given the opportunity in this exchange with Antoine to express her own latent aggression at the death of her mother and also the previously unfelt pleasure of turning passive into active. First, when the opportunity is offered to her, she declines. But then, after accepting it and acquiescing in it, she becomes, all of a sudden, in this new game—not of her initiating—the perpetrator instead of the victim. And she holds on to the gun for so long because she does not want to give up this sensation of power. Death is under *her* control now.

But, as always, the price of aggression is dear. And the price here is catastrophic. Ponette's response to hearing that she is her mother's killer is to retreat into total passivity and to wish to die. Of course, this wish, too, is complex and overdetermined because to die would be a way to rejoin her mother and identify with her. In the scene that follows, Matthias gets it out of her that it was Antoine who upset her so much, and he suggests that instead of Ponette killing herself or him killing her (which Ponette suggests) they should both seek out and kill Antoine! Thus, we witness the proliferation of aggression, the primitive solution of "kicking someone else," of passing the suffering on to another person. In this interchange, when Matthias is trying to comfort her this way, he makes the same suggestion her father had made on his departure for Lyon—namely, that tokens be exchanged—and Ponette gives him her father's watch in exchange for his Batman toy.

We arrive now at the final scenes of the film. A fascinating change occurs. With piano music playing in the background, Ponette, all dressed up in her winter coat, stands alone, expectantly, outside the door of the school. This time, however, unlike all the previous times when she has been waiting, she is waiting now not for her mother but for her papa. And yet something is nevertheless askew because, as it is suddenly pointed out to her, the day and time are incorrect. This is not in fact Friday, which is the day parents normally arrive to take their children away for the weekend. Ponette's father, therefore, will not be arriving. One of the teachers comes by and pulls her back indoors by the arm. Nevertheless, a dramatic alteration has taken place. We notice immediately that Ponette is now waiting for the *right* parent even though she is waiting on the *wrong* day. Later she tells Delphine that her mother actually came to her in a dream that night and she smelled like candy. "She hugged me," Ponette says, and then went away again. What we should notice here is the confluence of these two experiences—the dream of the mother and the waiting for the father—as well as the sensuousness of the dream imagery, the fact that it is the mother's smell and the memories of her embrace that are so sorely missed by the young child. We should note, also importantly, that these changes are able to occur—both the visitation of the mother in the dream and the waiting now for the living parent—only after the child's aggression has been expressed and her very normal wish to die has been articulated, spoken out loud and heard by a sympathetic friend.

Finally, we arrive at the culminating scenes of the movie. Ponette, as we have seen, has undergone a complex process involving both fragmentary testing of reality and fleeing from reality and withdrawal from the world. She has tried out various magical and religious strategies. She has made gifts and offerings, has tried endless waiting, incantations, trials, and prayers. She has shared her hopes with her peers but also tried keeping her deepest feelings secret from them. She has been able to relate both well and poorly to her surviving parent. She has suffered various physical ailments that have stood in symbolically for mental ones. She has experienced helplessness and aggression and the wish to die herself. Now, at the end of this extraordinary film, after trying in every way she can possibly imagine to reestablish her connection with her lost mother, she can be seen trudging along a country road with her backpack heading toward the cemetery itself. Alone, followed at a distance by the camera, only the music of the violin accompanies her.

She approaches her mother's grave, and then she sits down on the ground with her head resting against the gravestone. The earth beneath her is rich and brown and moist, and no grass has as yet begun to sprout over the recently dug plot. Ponette sits there silently. Her cast is all scruffy now, but we can still make out the drawing of the lion-dog. Ponette bends over the dirt and then, at first slowly but then faster and more frantically, she begins to rake it with her fingers, pulling the earth toward her in desperate gestures as if trying somehow to dig down under it to what lies beneath.

"*Maman!*" she cries out. "*Je suis là*" (I am here), and crying, broken-hearted, she lies down on her tummy in the earth of the grave site.

Suddenly, a figure appears, a lovely, graceful, spirited woman dressed warmly in a winter coat and scarf. Smiling at Ponette, she asks:

"Do I smell like candy?"

The effect of this apparition is hard to judge because viewers of the film will experience it differently. To me, it brought, on first viewing, instant tears. It seemed such a patiently long awaited, sought for, and well-deserved reward! So exquisitely right to allow the child—at last—to have her wish come true.

As her mother takes Ponette by the hand now and kisses her, they walk briskly and play together and tease one another, and her mother tells her a little about how the accident happened but only in a way that resonates with the child's fantasies and needs.

"When I realized I was dying I let go," she tells Ponette. "I didn't think of you. I was mean. But, as I went under, I heard you calling me. . . . Last night you held me."

Ponette, utterly speechless at first, gradually begins to respond with incredulity, then wonder, then utter joy. They run and laugh, holding hands.

"Tomorrow Daddy will take you and you'll laugh all day," her mother says. And then she adds:

"Nobody likes a neglectful child. What is a neglectful child?" to which Ponette answers,

"A child who forgets to laugh?"

And, her mother asks jauntily:

"Why are you alive?" and then answers her own question: "To try everything!" She goes on: "Try everything, and then you can die."

And later:

"Happy spirits like your mother never die."

Ponette, seeking maternal comfort as well as playfulness, complains that she is cold, and her mother immediately gives her her red sweater, which she has thoughtfully brought along. And then, her lip beginning to tremble, Ponette asks her whether she will stay. Her mother answers sternly:

"You know that I am dead. My head hit the steering wheel. Everything was broken."

And now Ponette begins to fight back the tears. Again her mother reminds her of her father:

"Go and be happy with him," she bids her. "I am sad when you are not happy with him. Don't forget I love you."

With this, she explains that she must leave and refuses Ponette's pleas that she might be able to hide and remain with her. She tells Ponette to turn around now and go and see her papa. But the little girl, trying to be brave, cannot refrain from asking just one more time:

"Do you love me for real?"

"Oh, yes!" her mother answers passionately, standing in silhouette on the path with the wind blowing in her hair and her scarf.

"Go find Papa."

Ponette turns back, takes a few steps away, and then, like Orpheus, cannot help turning her head around. But this time all is emptiness.

Suddenly a car appears, and her father is kneeling beside her asking her what she is doing there and where she has been. She tells him that her mother has come back and talked to her and that she wasn't scared and she gave her her red sweater. This time, in an exquisite moment of truly empathic parenting, her father valorizes her fantasy.

"She was right to," he says.

"But," Ponette tells him, "she is never coming back."

"Well," he replies, philosophically, "She can't keep making these round trips."

Holding Ponette's hand, he walks with her as, with her eyes shining, she utters the final words of the film:

"She told me to learn to be happy."

Thus, we see in detail how one film depicts a child's mourning with extraordinary brilliance and delicacy. By studying it, we can better understand the difficulties and complexities of parent-child relations at such a time. We are able, by the end, to observe at least two additional phenomena, and I should add that these are noted by Wolfenstein in her aforementioned writings. One of them is the gradual transfer of trust, love, and dependency from a deceased to a surviving parent so that the child, believing in the living parent, need not consume so much mental energy holding desperately to images of the one who has died. Second, we see here an illustration of the notion that at the end of a successful mourning process what we witness is at least a partial severing of memory from hope. The child, in other words, has come to be able to live and go onward with loving recollections of her lost parent but without the continuing burdensome fantasy that the lost parent will return and without a corresponding withdrawal from the world that such a fantasy requires. These goals, of course, are never fully realized, either in this film or in any person's real life, but they are worthy ideals.

As a final postscript, I want to say that the cast—with its lion-dog drawing—on Ponette's arm is never, throughout the film, removed. This fact gives us a clue as to the duration of time that is meant to be represented here, for the cast on the broken arm of a four year old would not remain in place more than three to four months, a period far too short for all that we have seen were it to have occurred in real time. Thus, it is important to remember that in dealing with works of art we must always allow for the encapsulation and abridgement of time. Instead of the traditional epigram, "*ars longa, vita brevis*" (art is long and time is fleeting), we must, in a situation like this, when we are dealing with the exigencies of mourning and with psychological processes in general, and with the succeeding chapters in this book, amend that saying and substitute its corollary, namely, "*vita longa, ars brevis*" (life is long but works of art are brief).

The Boy-Girl

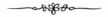

If they see
breasts and long hair coming
they call it woman,

if beard and whiskers
they call it man:

but, look, the self that hovers
in between
is neither man
nor woman.

—TENTH-CENTURY SAIVITE
DEVOTEE, INDIA

I don't want to change,
but I want them to love me.

—BERLINER, *MA VIE EN ROSE*

A child's fantasy life proliferates, occasionally, like vines and leaves on some fast-growing ivy plant, which, almost before our eyes, climbs helter-skelter up red brick walls and expands in all directions; it overruns the sociocultural scaffolding that supports it. In the previous chapter, we saw how a child like Ponette clings tenaciously to her imaginings, and we watched as significant adults in her life struggle to contain and modify them. How do we foster such children and

Ma vie en rose (1997, France), directed by Alain Berliner.
Shown: Georges Du Fresne. (Courtesy of Photofest.)

protect them from harm when their inner lives prove pertinaciously intractable?

Here we meet a boy of seven whose wishes and beliefs, when acted out, also alter other people's lives, as well as, of course, his own. Ludovic Fabre (of Belgian filmmaker Alain Berliner's 1997 *Ma vie en rose* [My Life in Pink], released in French with English subtitles) wants to be, and believes himself to be, a girl. Shimmering pink dresses, pastel-colored flowers, glittering heart shapes and stardust, earrings, makeup, long hair, and shoes with elevated heels enchant him. He wants to partake of them. He wants them for and of and on himself rather than as objects contemplated wistfully from afar. Without meaning to, he challenges norms regarding the preferences of little boys, and then, as he does so, the kaleidoscopic patterns all around him start to shift. His actions give rise to an escalating series of ruptures and realignments that he, owing to his naïveté and the strength of his wishes, cannot fathom. He wants simply to follow up and pursue what attracts him. Hurt and often bewildered by the shocked reactions he produces on the part of those he loves and in whose good graces he wants to be, he tells a therapist at one point that he does *not* want to change but he *does* want to be loved. In so saying, this seven-year-old child brilliantly sums up a fundamental element of the human condition: civilization and its discontents. Or, as artist Louise Bourgeois once stunningly asked: how *can* one be oneself and still be likable?

Eventually, Ludovic's wish to be a girl derails the everyday life of his family. His behavior vexes relationships not only among his father, mother, and siblings but also among his playmates and neighbors. When it disastrously impacts his father's employment (his dad is eventually dismissed from his job), it places the very security of his family at risk. Only his maternal grandmother, Elisabeth, who fancies herself forever young and indulges in daydreams of her own, seems able to identify uncomplicatedly with him. Throughout the film, this grandmother, or "Granny" as she is called *à l'anglaise*, remains unthreatened by Ludovic's longings.

Arriving on camera early in the film, she opens the door of her car with a flourish and bursts out, affectionately greeting her grandsons and instructing them to call her "Elisabeth" instead of Grandmother.

Close your eyes, she tells little Ludovic at one point, and you can be whatever you wish. For her, this means repossessing a sleek body and unblemished skin; for the boy, it brings visions of verdant meadows strewn with iridescent plastic daisies over which a resplendent airborne icon named Pam floats trailing long blonde curls, her tiny waist encased in rosy, filmy fabrics. Reminiscent of his sister's Barbie doll, Ludovic's Pam soars gracefully over chartreuse valleys and hills surmounted by Styrofoam clouds. This imagery, recurrent throughout the film, gives form to the little boy's longings and shows us how, via graphic elements drawn selectively from the culture around him, he—in the imagination of the filmmaker—both evades and expands on the limited role assigned to him.

Of course, in subtle and unremarkable ways, a similar sort of leakage of fantasy happens to all of us more or less. Like Ludovic Fabre, we inflate our iridescent daydreams and waft them about with invisible wands as if they were bubbles. They evaporate into the atmosphere we breathe and are inhaled by those around us. They are the "pipe dreams" of Eugene O'Neill's *The Iceman Cometh*. But how are parents to handle a child who outrages everyone without being able to fathom why his predilections, which seem so natural to him, are deemed outlandish by everyone else?

Ma vie en rose recounts this story of Ludo, as he is affectionately called in diminutive, who both longs to be, and believes he is, of the opposite sex by offering a progression of deftly crafted scenes that sharpen, one by one, our perception of the ever-widening ripples of reaction to his socially unacceptable behavior. We watch with fascination and dismay as the ripples expand beyond his loving but perplexed family to encompass his scandalized neighborhood and school administration.

Never does Berliner "explain" his protagonist's cross-gender identification. Initially deeming this a fault in the film, I have come, over many viewings, to regard it as one of the work's greatest strengths. Berliner has balked at giving in to clichés and stereotypes. He plants hints but then yanks them out by the roots like weeds, and this stubborn refusal on his part to derive Ludo's "problem" from simplistic sources mirrors Ludo's own stubborn refusal to capitulate to the notion that his ideas about himself are wrongheaded and that he must give them up. We are introduced to an appealing, well-loved child who delights in girlish clothing, feminine-coded colors, props, and toys. He plays happily with dolls, wears his hair in a pageboy bob, cross-dresses, experiments at one point with putting his pants on backward with the fly opening at the rear, attempts to pee while sitting on a toilet seat, and stages a pretend wedding with another little boy in which he himself plays the bride. How do we as the audience react?

Rather than deriving these behaviors from parental peculiarities— rather than implicating the mother, for example, by portraying her as overly seductive and provocative or blaming the father by painting him as unavailable, pusillanimous, cold, and/or violent—a tack that might well have been taken by a less sophisticated director, Berliner pulls back, sagely, from any trite attribution of cause. Instead of demonizing one or another of the child's parents, he accords them the utmost in compassion and humor. Indeed, Hanna and Pierre Fabre, Ludo's mother and father, are cast as warm, caring, and devoted parents. Ingenuously, they express their affection for one another and their four children, of whom Ludo is the youngest. When, in outbursts of helpless frustration at Ludo's recalcitrance and their own incomprehension of him and inability to cope, they turn momentarily against each other, we are shocked because such moments diverge from their normally benign interactions.

As an example of Hanna's mothering, we find, well on in the film, a scene during which Ludo's big sister Zoe falls ill with stomach cramps, and it soon becomes clear that she is undergoing her first menstrual period. Hanna, at this significant moment in her daughter's life, offers a response that typifies her personality and her parenting.

"I am very proud of you," she says gently to Zoe, while comforting and soothing her. She offers the girl a warm towel for her pain and also gives her daughter permission to stay out a bit later with her boyfriend now that "she is a real lady."

Later on in these pages we shall meet another pubescent girl, Jamaica Kincaid's title character Annie John, whose mother greets the identical news on her daughter's part with what feels to the girl like rejection, lack of warmth, appropriation, and a stark refusal to acknowledge any physical pain at all. Hanna's warmth toward Zoe, on the other hand, is replicated in her relations with her husband, her older boys, and, importantly, Ludo.

How then to account for this child? How can we comprehend him? His parents are stymied. Their other children, the two sons and Zoe, whom Ludo especially adores, seem perfectly content to function within their respective, conventionally assigned gender roles, as are Hanna and Pierre. Why is Ludo different? At one point, Hanna pleads:

"We have no idea what goes on in his head."

When Ludo is taken in desperation, finally, to a well-meaning but rather passive and ineffectual psychologist, this woman, after a number of play therapy sessions and several abortive attempts to engage him in dialogue, both alone and with his parents, ends up telling Pierre and Hanna that she can do nothing further for him. Her inconclusive treatment of him thus abruptly stops, and the frustrated parents, who have placed characteristically unrealistic hopes in her, feel aggrieved and defeated by what appears to them a premature termination. They even sense betrayal in her failure to normalize and thereby "save" their son. The psychologist's "failure," however, contributes to the overall ethos of the film. I read it as signifying that we are meant not so much to question the competence or good faith of the psychologist (as do Ludo's parents) but rather to ask ourselves whether indeed the notion that anything is "wrong" with Ludo makes sense at all and whether in fact he needs a "cure."

At one point early on, the psychologist asks Hanna and Pierre to tell her about their fantasies before the child's birth: had they hoped for a boy or a girl? Meanwhile, Ludo, who is playing quietly on the floor nearby, is privy to the adults' conversation. No doubt the psychologist's question is motivated by widespread notions that parental hopes and dreams about their unborn children have momentous untold consequences, a point we shall explore later on in these pages with reference to Doris Lessing's novel *The Fifth Child*. The Fabres' first reply to her question is that they had wanted, simply, a healthy baby. Quickly, however, they amend this answer to confess that they *had* actually hoped for a girl in order to balance the existing two-to-one gender ratio among their older children. They add, immediately, however, that when their little boy, Ludo, was born they adored him from the start.

Listening in on this dialogue, Ludo feels vindicated and affirmed. Curious to understand more, he goes quickly to his beloved Zoe, who is now studying biology among her subjects at the local *collège*, and he asks her to explain to him the difference between baby boys and girls. Zoe consults her textbook and reports a bit of cursory information on X and Y chromosomes, sufficient for Ludo to concoct an ingenious theory about his unique origins. He comes up with the notion that his "other X" was lost somehow—thrown accidentally into a trash bin, perhaps—and that it will resurface, at which point he will turn (back) into a girl. From this point on, he calls himself a *garçon-fille*, "a boy-girl."

53

Berliner, however, downplays the parental interchange with the psychologist by giving it a slightly parodic tone. The parents' answer, after all, is just precisely what the psychologist had been *expecting* to hear and just precisely what we as the audience have been *programmed* to hear. As such, it is made to seem both obvious and trivial.

For, in fact, there are, in this film, no simple reasons, no pat answers, and no cures. We are drawn in and invited to share the plight of one family and child. We are presented with Ludo just as he is. We are asked to watch carefully and take note of all that happens. In this way, the task, importantly, becomes ours. We, too, like all the on-camera characters, must come to terms with what we encounter. We must make our own sense of it and find our solutions—if we can—to this riddle of a supposedly deviant child. When, in fact, I have screened *Ma vie en rose* for my undergraduates, they have tended to take it exactly this way, that is to say, on its own terms. Invariably, some weep; few if any come away unmoved by Ludo's plight. The film puts them into a reflective mood, and a number of them, even those who come from traditionally oriented religious homes where gender-coded distinctions are strictly observed, express solidarity with the little boy. One or two of them even reveal, hesitantly, their own now remembered and long disavowed secret longings to be what they are not. Such moments enable us to glimpse how art, with its delicate displacements, lets us see more than what is apparent, lets us gaze through the surface of a work toward private inner vistas of our own.

Our story begins when Ludo's family has just moved into a new neighborhood with manicured lawns and well-maintained homes that look almost like imitations of American suburban dwellings, an observation that proves disconcerting when we discover, all too soon, how bigoted its inhabitants can be. The Fabres have decided to host a housewarming party to introduce themselves to their neighbors. Our first images onscreen are of women preening for this event. Flowery spring dresses are back-zipped by husbands amid cheerful banter and flurries of conjugal teasing and flirtatiousness. The initial moments of the film, therefore, establish as its touchstone a communal norm of fully subscribed, well-entrenched heterosexuality.

In the afternoon sunlight, with neighbors standing about outdoors in and among festive tables, Pierre, our host, when all the guests have assembled on his lawn, introduces his family one by one. Hanna, who wears a striking crimson sheath, cannot at the last minute find her matching shoes and complains about the uncomfortable ones she has been forced to wear instead. After being introduced to the guests by Pierre as "the prettiest one," along with his two older sons, to whom he similarly accords apt but facetious epithets, Hanna calls loudly for Ludo and her daughter Zoe, both of whom are missing.

What we next see, however, are not the two absent children. Rather, the camera zooms in on a blond Barbie doll. Next a pair of dressy red ladies shoes with stacked heels. Feet are inserted into them that are far too small. Above the feet, we gradually make out the trimmed hem of a glossy, rose-colored party dress. The camera now shows us a hand mirror rimmed in pink in which a child's face is reflected. A little girl applies dark ruby lipstick very inexpertly, and, after admiring herself, she adorns herself with dangly teardrop jade earrings. Assuming we are witnessing the primping of the Fabres' daughter Zoe, we sense something indefinable that seems vaguely awry. The scene, in fact, is our introduction not to Zoe but to Ludo, who is upstairs preparing himself to come down to the party. Having "borrowed" his sister's dress and his mother's missing red shoes, as well as her makeup and earrings, he now cautiously makes his way downstairs, trying hard not to trip.

When he appears in the doorway of the house after Hanna has once again called for Zoe, the guests—and we ourselves as spectators of the film—believe we are finally meeting the Fabres' missing daughter. But then, looming behind him in pigtails and play clothes, and wearing a disgruntled expression (presumably because she could not find her party dress), we notice Zoe herself who, rising up behind her little brother, gives the lie immediately to his elaborate masquerade.

The guests are no more startled than Hanna and Pierre themselves: *a boy dressed as a girl!* But Pierre suavely rescues the situation by introducing Ludo as "the jokey one," thus saving face and protecting his son while managing to assuage the anxiety of the assembled guests, who stare in disbelief at this flamboyantly cross-dressed apparition. The celebration must not be spoiled. It is worthy of note that, while momentarily stunned by Ludo's caper, neither of his parents manifests any anger at him. Even Zoe seems quickly mollified even though it is her dress that has been filched. The Fabre family thus pulls together and presents a united front, an instinctive bonding, which proves constant for them throughout the story even as the situation around them deteriorates.

Many a father would be mortified if his son, even if only seven years of age, appeared in public cross-dressed. Pierre, however, in deflecting it as a "joke," helps to calm himself as well as everyone else. What he tells his guests, however, is patently untrue: Ludo is not joking. We can tell this from the pure, intense joy with which the child was contemplating his reinvented face in the mirror. He is not clowning. He does not want to be laughed at. He wants to be seen as, and admired as, a *girl.* Moreover, a powerful feeling of rightness and a sense of entitlement render him devoid of remorse—not only for pretending to be a girl but also for having borrowed his mother's and sister's belongings without asking for them. He is never reprimanded, incidentally, for this unauthorized borrowing. Ethical considerations completely succumb in this scene, as in the film at large, to questions of propriety. Boys do *not* dress as girls. This seems to be a doctrine that overrides the prohibition against taking something that belongs to someone else. I wish to pause here and focus on this point because it seems remarkable and may lead us to further insight.

Later on in the story, Ludo engages in other acts of unauthorized and even forbidden borrowing, acts that land him (and his family) in serious trouble. One climactic moment occurs when, in a school production of *Snow White,* Ludo locks his classmate and neighbor, another seven-year-old child named Sophie, who has been chosen to play the part of the heroine, in the girls' bathroom in order to steal her costume. He then proceeds to go onstage himself in her place, an act that results not only in his expulsion from school but, even more catastrophically, in his father's dismissal from his job. Yet at no point is Ludo's ethical transgression raised and addressed as such. It is always and ever the threatening impropriety of his transgender pretense (as it is deemed) and his acting out that preoccupy the adults around him.

Thus, a pattern is established from the start, in the very first scenes, which obtains throughout the film and presents us with a model I wish to question. Hanna's feet, after all, hurt because she has been wearing the wrong shoes at the party, and Zoe has been prevented from being introduced to the guests in her own special dress. Yet these trespasses on Ludo's part, these transgressions against the rights of others, elicit no comment. Why?

Let's try to understand by looking first at the symbolism of hair. When small children (who are growing up in the contemporary West) want to differentiate the sexes visually, one marker they commonly use is hair: long hair for girls and women, short hair for boys and men. Hanna, trained as a *coiffeuse,* styles and cuts the hair of every member of her family; it is clear, therefore, from the start that she has actively colluded with Ludo in his feminine pageboy bob. He wears his hair like a girl, in other words, with the family's acquiescence and approval. Later, as tragic events precipitate the family toward their expulsion from the community, Hanna, to avert a repetition of the horrors they have endured, cuts Ludo's hair. This is a key scene in the film. Surrounded by the entire family, she performs this perfectly normal, everyday act, which, suddenly in this altered context of the film, becomes barbaric. Tears stream down the child's contorted face. The other children look on stricken with compassion, and Hanna, crying herself, can barely steel herself to perform the act. Zoe, who is unable to watch, flees from the room. For many of my students, this scene— when we view the film together in class—proves the hardest one to bear and the one that brings tears to them as well.

Initially, Ludo's family does not see his behavior as a problem. It and he simply do not register as trouble. After all, they adore him. He is their baby, the darling of the household, and, in consequence, they are exquisitely tolerant of him. As far as they are concerned, he can do no wrong. His actions become intolerable *only* when they provoke conflicts between themselves as a family and the outside world. We have seen that, when he takes Hanna's shoes and Zoe's dress, there is a tacit acknowledgment that, since his having asked permission in advance would have been met with a negative, the secrecy was unavoidable. As such, it is not addressed. Tolerance like this, within the family, however, while gracious and admirable, brings with it a tangle of problems later on. Most saliently, familial tolerance of conduct deemed deviant in the outside world cannot protect any child for very long. Indeed, it cannot protect a family itself for very long from the prejudices of society and its constraints.

It is worthwhile considering, moreover, the links between tolerance and obliviousness. By accepting Ludo uncritically, Hanna and Pierre also protect and hide from themselves. They avoid facing whatever unresolved issues they, individually and as a couple, might be harboring in regard to gender. Thus, when they pull back from addressing the disjunction between ethical and gender issues, they collude with Ludo. Surely, after all, it ought to be possible to talk with a child about the offense of appropriating another person's possessions without confusing that conversation with a different conversation about what might be appropriate for boys but not girls and vice versa. Ludo, swept away by the immediacy and power of his wishes, does not notice that his sister and mother may have their own equally valid wishes—wishes, in this case, to wear their own garments. Seven year olds, in fact, do have considerable capacity for empathy (see, for example, Paley 1999; and Gopnick 2009), but Ludo, in this case, seems utterly oblivious of having inconvenienced his mother and disappointed his sister. No one, furthermore, helps him to expand his awareness along these lines. A potentially valuable teaching moment is lost.

Likewise, later on, when Ludo locks Sophie in the bathroom at school and appropriates her Snow White apparel, he does so under the sway of what feels to him a sudden rush of overpowering desire. *Her* sense of betrayal at being robbed of her moment of glory onstage counts for naught where he is concerned. Yet, even at this point in the story, while the entire school is present as audience for the play, and all are dumbfounded, transfixed with amazement to see Ludo's face appearing instead of Sophie's as Snow White, the moral transgression is sidelined. Public outrage focuses exclusively on the gender-bending.

In reflecting on this conflation of realms that are eminently separable, we find that self-protection on the part of adults once again proves a powerful motivating force in the handling of young children. If Ludo, instead of secretly pilfering, were to have come openly to his parents and asked them to buy dolls and jewelry for him, if he had begged them for permission to walk outdoors cross-dressed or to attend school in girls' clothing, if he had asked his teacher for permission to play the part of Snow White in the play, the apparent tolerance and obliviousness of the adults might have shut down with a bang. By not being open in his desires, Ludo does not make them confront the deepest levels of their own anxiety, their own fears about being different. By ignoring his unauthorized borrowing, by not addressing it, they can sustain a level of superficial tolerance while at the same time evading conflicts within themselves and any major soul-searching. Not only that. Ludo, too, on some level, becomes tacitly aware of this dynamic, as children often are. His clandestine behavior thus serves—reflexively—as a way of protecting them from themselves (see, apropos, Miller 1981). Whatever is negative and critical can be projected onto the outside world.

Yet, as noted further on in these pages, parental abnegation and self-protection, undertaken unawares and with the kindliest and most loving of conscious motives, as well as with the unwitting complicity of the child involved, cannot help but result in grave problems down the line. As a social unit, bound inextricably to a larger whole, the family—when it ignores or tolerates behavior that is unacceptable to that larger whole—sets off, sooner or later, reactions and repercussions that, at some point, can no longer be contained solely within it. Every family, embedded, as it must be, in a wider context, wrestles with that context and the influence and control it exerts.

Ma vie en rose traces the negotiations of such embeddedness to show us, vividly, how hard it is to inoculate ourselves against what we superficially oppose and how much we, in spite of ourselves, participate in it. My students ache when Hanna cuts Ludo's hair because she is giving in. She is becoming one with the forces arraigned against him. By not finding any way to address the ethical aspects of his behavior early on, his parents set him up and set themselves up for what happens. With loving intentions, they support him in the present but pave the way for transgressions with ever more dire consequences. Cosseted at home, pressed by his desires, the little boy is not led toward an appreciation of the feelings of others or toward compromise formations by parents who, in keeping with their own prior socialization and emotional needs, must bypass the opportunity he presents to them both to learn and to teach.

There is at the party an unforgettable moment of perfect bliss when Granny, aka Elisabeth, who is the self-appointed disc jockey of the hour, starts up some lilting, highly spirited music and then begins dancing wildly and blithely to it with Ludo. Hanna joins quickly in, so that, in seconds, the child finds himself pressed blissfully between his mother and his undulating grandmother, and the camera records him beatifically smiling, embraced by both women, ecstatically and rhythmically cavorting in this triad to the music.

Apropos of this scene, a beloved American record album from the 1970s and its accompanying illustrated songbook for children— *William's Doll* from *Free to Be You and Me* (1972)—which touts the message that anyone, whether boy or girl, can achieve whatever he or she wishes, also prominently features a grandmother who supports a little boy's wishes. In this case, the wish is to have a doll, and it is the grandmother who buys the coveted toy. In *Free to Be You and Me,* however, the grandmother gives somewhat different reasons for her support of the boy than those that motivate Ludo's grandmother. Elisabeth's credo, in the Berliner film, seems to be that children should be permitted to act out their transgressive wishes as a kind of safety valve. In this way, they will soon tire of them, and the antics will subside, diminish in value, and eventually fade away. Such tactics, parenthetically, are pursued with success by a pair of wise parents in *Bread and Jam for Frances,* by Russell and Lillian Hoban (1964), a psychologically astute picture book in which a little girl (badger) is permitted to eat nothing but her favorite food for as long as she likes. Eventually, of course, she begs for variety. William's grandmother, by way of contrast, views children's play as role preparation. Focusing on the adaptive aspects of a boy's wish for a doll, she points to the fact that caring for dolls in childhood may serve to groom a small boy for fatherhood in the future.

Thus, the two grandmothers adduce different yet complementary

reasons for their indulgence, reasons founded on alternative construc-
tions of the function of play in childhood. One grandmother views play
as a siphon so that the child can make believe he has and is what is de-
sired but proscribed in reality. The other grandmother sees play as a
proving ground: a make-believe practice for future adult tasks. In these
different but not unrelated starting points, each grandparent grounds
her own affectionate, broad-minded permissiveness, and, as we shall
see later on, a similar attitude appears in these pages in the character
of Lena Younger (Mama) in the chapter "In My Mother's House" on
Lorraine Hansberry's *A Raisin in the Sun*. There Mama's leniency toward Travis, her grandson, is equally adoring and equally emblematic
of the ways in which a three-generational divide can foster uncon-
flicted identification, acceptance, and pleasurable indulgence.

Among the neighbors at the housewarming party is Pierre's portly
new boss, Albert, who attends with his prim, rather dull wife Lisette
and their sullen son Jerome who, as it turns out, will be at school with
Ludo. Jerome spies one of the earrings Ludo wears at the party, which
has fallen unnoticed to the ground. Secretly, he retrieves it and brings
it to school, where he reveals it clandestinely to Ludo. The boys, sharing this forbidden secret, instantly become intrigued with one another
and, seeking friendship, they arrange a play date at Jerome's house just
on the afternoon when Lisette, who is a dressmaker, happens to be
hemming a frock for Hanna. The background scene and interchange
between the two mothers illumines the ensuing contact between their
sons. It sets up a contrast between the attractive, ebullient Hanna, who
confidently insists on having her skirts pinned ever higher, and the
placid, inhibited Lisette, whose sense of propriety finds expression
only in her scandalized eyes, which she quickly averts.

Jerome, in showing off his house to Ludo, explains that his sister's
room is off-limits because, as he says, "*elle est partie*," a phrase that literally means "she has gone away" but that serves, we soon discover, as a
euphemism, in this case, for "she has died." Peering inside the forbidden chamber, Ludo feels an immediate thrill of pleasure at its feminine contents as the camera pans slowly over the little girl's rosy-col-
ored decor, frilly toys, and dolls. When he disobediently opens her

closet door to expose a satiny pink dress adorned with a ruby heart, *les jeux sont faits*. In minutes, he has donned this dress. Soon, at his urging, the children have rigged up a make-believe wedding ceremony in the dead girl's room. They pose her teddy bear on a shelf as the vicar while Jerome performs the role of the groom and Ludo becomes, of course, the blushing bride.

Lisette, having finished pinning Hanna's hems, comes wandering through the halls looking for the boys and pauses momentarily before her deceased daughter's bedroom, where she unexpectedly hears voices. When she peers in and sees what is happening, she collapses in a faint. Hanna, horrified, in large part because Lisette is the wife of her husband's boss, grabs Ludo firmly by the hand and jerks him away from the house. Their little girl is dead, she tells him; how could you? But Ludo protests that he did not know. Jerome said she was "gone," and how was he to know that this meant "dead"?

Then, in a flash, we are flying in the sky with the magical iconic figure of the long-haired, blonde Pam, Ludo's alter ego, who is wafting streams of magical stardust into the air that shelter him (and Jerome) from the wrath of all uncomprehending adults. Eventually, Hanna reproves Ludo by informing him authoritatively that boys do not marry other boys; Ludo, however, confidently replies:

"I'll be a girl," to which Hanna responds with mingled resignation and pride:

"You are stubborn (*têtu*)—just like your mother."

In this instant, the director Berliner gives another wink to the truism that little boys like Ludo identify exclusively with their mothers. But Hanna is no Pam, and Ludo, as we shall see, is deeply attached to his father.

At the dinner table that night, Pierre is visibly angry, not because of Ludo's inclinations per se, as we already know, but angry out of fear that his child's behavior might cause professional complications for him. He is worried about the security of his new job and the family's welfare. When he voices these concerns by pointing out that Jerome's dad is his boss, Hanna defends Ludo, and Pierre, feeling alienated and unjustly maligned, leaves the dinner table in high dudgeon to go out to the garden where he tries to calm himself by doing chin-ups on the trellis.

"You deal with it," is his parting shot to Hanna.

Ludo, however, instantly slips from his chair and follows his father outdoors. Silently approaching the distraught Pierre, he places his small hand in the larger one, and, their arms around each other, they slowly return to the house together.

In this way, Berliner makes us keenly aware that Ludo is deeply attached to and identified with *both* parents and that no simplistic theory can explain him away.

In school, Ludo and Jerome have been sitting side by side at their desks. After the "wedding," Jerome raises his hand during class and asks their teacher to switch his seat. When the teacher wants to know why, he answers, in front of all the other children, that he will go to hell if he does not move away from Ludo. Burning with shame, Ludo runs out of the classroom in tears to find Zoe, who comforts him. Similar scenes, we should note, in which a child (who is deemed "other") is publicly humiliated in a school classroom occur in films where the aggressor is not another child but a benighted teacher. Here that is not the case. Ludo's open-minded young French teacher clearly wants to contain the damage and shelter him. Her slender efforts cannot, however, hold sway against the powerful forces arraigned against him and fomented by the community at large. Eventually she, too, turns against him when he ruins the performance of *Snow White* that she has worked so hard with the other children to produce. Her anger at Ludo at this point is on behalf of Sophie and the others, who, she apparently feels, have been hurt by his inconsiderate behavior. Until this moment, she does her best to defend him.

It is worthwhile to note and understand the precise moment when each of the other significant figures in Ludo's life finally breaks down and gets angry with him and why. Pierre, as we have seen, first expresses dismay when he realizes his job may be at risk. For the safety of the family, he wants Ludo to conform. After the school play when twenty parents sign a petition for his son's expulsion, he *is* eventually sacked by Jerome's father. Brokenly, Pierre arrives home to announce the news, but he is no longer angry at Ludo. He is heartsore and dev-astated. Now it is Hanna who becomes enraged.

When the little boy asks whether the loss of his father's job is his fault, Pierre replies:

"No. People are shit. Bloody hypocrites."

Contradicting him in a fury, Hanna replies:

"I'm sick of hypocrisy. It is your fault we're here" (she tells Ludo).

Pierre at that juncture, to palliate her anger, quotes the grand-mother's words:

"Maybe he'll outgrow it."

But later, when the psychologist stops her sessions, Hanna again ac-cuses Ludo:

"You have messed up our lives," she tells him.

Thus, anger at the child seems to occur when each adult perceives himself or herself at risk personally and vulnerable as a result of the child's behavior. Pierre foresees catastrophe and expresses his resent-ment in advance. Hanna, on the other hand, recognizes the full impact only after damage has been done. This is when she flares up. Instead of taking Ludo's part as she has up to now, she makes it clear from this moment on that she has lost her capacity to do so.

Even earlier, just after Ludo's expulsion from his neighborhood school, we see her standing on a street corner with him waiting impa-tiently for a city bus that will take him to his new school in a distant, tougher neighborhood, a large public institution where, in fact, he will soon be roughed up and actually threatened with castration by loutish bullies in a sports locker room. Previously, all the neighborhood chil-dren had been driven to school in their parents' private cars, and Hanna is now pained and sorely aggrieved at Ludo for the inconve-nience he has caused her with these new arrangements. When the at-tack against him occurs, moreover, in the new school, it takes place in front of Ludo's older brothers, who fail to defend him. In cowardice and fear, they turn against one another instead of against the strangers who are brutalizing their little brother.

The behavior of these older brothers at this juncture illustrates a dy-namic we have previously observed, namely, the readiness of others to disidentify with Ludo as soon as his relations with the extrafamilial world turn sour. His brothers, despite their demonstrable love for him, cannot bear to be associated with him when others turn against him. Shame and fear trump their loyalty and affection. Ludo disappears after this attack at school, and when he does not reappear for many hours the family is racked with anxiety and guilt. At length, he is found by Hanna. She discovers him in the garage hidden in a closed freezer as if it were a coffin, and the image on the screen evokes, once again, *Snow White*. His brothers blame each other for what happened under their eyes; neither accepts responsibility. Their inability to translate *intra*familial feelings into matching *extra*familial conduct can be traced directly to the same roots as their parents' inability to separate ethical from gender issues. The Fabre family possesses strength, love, and cohesiveness, but these qualities come at the prohibitive cost of developing effective strategies for dealing with the incursions of the outside world.

Zoe, as we have seen, adores her little brother. She treats him with kindness, compassion, and forbearance. Until, that is, he does something that upsets her and calls into question her own gender issues. When, as recounted earlier, she suffers the typical pains associated with a girl's first menstrual period, Ludo, all curiosity, wants to know why she does not feel well and what this has to do with her being a "lady." Unbidden, he comes into her room to question her. Zoe, at this moment, does not want to talk with him. Physically uncomfortable, her attention is focused, understandably, on herself and her own momentously changing body. She has no patience for a little brother. She wants to be left alone. Firmly, she tells Ludo that only girls get their periods (*les règles*), and then she shoos him away. Not, however, before Ludo grabs a chance to say that *he* will get *his* period too! This truly infuriates Zoe, who slams her door on him.

What is it about this moment that upsets her and makes her turn so uncharacteristically against Ludo? Beyond feeling unwell and thus weakened (her defenses are down), she needs to claim the right to be fully present to her own new life experience and not share it with an inquisitive seven-year-old brother. But this is not all.

Ludo, up to this point, has been attracted to femininity by what he fancies as its external glitter and shine. He sees it as shimmer, amusement, and delight (*ma vie en rose!*). Menstruation, however, is none of the above, and Zoe resents him for that; in other words, it is as though Ludo, by pretending to be a girl, can borrow her party dresses and partake of all the pleasurable aspects of femininity; whereas, she, the *real* girl, must also endure its pains. Whatever gender questions or confusions a growing girl may have about herself, the advent of her first menses assigns her irrevocably to the female sex and thus both opens and closes a door in her own fantasy life. Zoe, of course, is not conscious of such thoughts. Ludo has not suddenly morphed for her into a sham or an impostor, but now, at this turning point in her own life, a new gulf opens not only between herself and him but between herself and her former self as a little girl. She cannot explain to Ludo what it means to be female, nor does she want to, but she knows, as she did not know before, that there is a cleavage between them that he cannot comprehend. This makes her turn away. She wants and needs to be alone.

Eventually, the community's bigotry triumphs. Ugly graffiti appears on the Fabres' family garage walls, Pierre is beaten up, and, in a wrenching scene, as I have described, Hanna cuts Ludo's hair.

When a new job turns up in faraway Clermont-Ferrand, the family readies itself to leave. They bid farewell in a touching scene to the grandmother, Elisabeth, whose inability to kiss them good-bye, while bitter for all, upholds her preservation of a fantasy world in which the adverse aspects of reality are kept at bay. Moving day, furthermore, is characterized by Ludo's ongoing fantasy life. He imagines lovely ornamented dresses and other items of clothing cascading down from the sky and falling at the feet of Jerome and his dour parents, Albert and Lisette, who stand impassively outdoors in front of their house while the departing Fabre family car pulls poignantly away. Shortly before this, in a spiteful moment of sweet revenge, Hanna deliberately and brazenly kisses Albert long and hard on his mouth in the street in front of a horrified Lisette, and, when he—in shock—calls Hanna a demon as she sashays victoriously away, she turns back toward him and makes malicious gleeful faces, rather like a wicked child.

Their new community turns out to be considerably less privileged than the previous one, with houses built one adjacent to the next and no green lawns. Hanna, who takes the comedown in their fortunes hard, blames Ludo. Crestfallen, he wanders through the desolate neighborhood with his odd short hair until by chance he meets a girl called Christine, a stocky tomboy, who pelts him with her slingshot by way of introduction. Haltingly, they become friends, and then, at her masquerade birthday party, Christine secretly persuades Ludo, when he arrives dressed as a musketeer, to change costumes with her. Ludo is reluctant, dubious, and very worried. Christine insists, however, claiming persuasively that it is *her* birthday.

Hanna arrives. Seeing Ludo dressed once again as a girl, she loses all control of herself. Raising her voice and her arm, in front of everyone, she strikes and rebukes him:

"You are bent on ruining our lives."

We realize, of course, that she is terrified. Once again, her family will be ostracized and forced to undergo a repetition of what they have just endured. Christine's mother, however, gentle and warm, tries to calm her down by reminding her that children often do such things and, in any case, the idea was her daughter's, not Ludo's. Ludo, humiliated and rejected now by his own mother, runs away. Hanna races out the door in pursuit of him. Calling his name frantically, she searches for him up and down the streets.

Eventually, exhausted, she stops along a nearby roadway where she spies a billboard with a flamboyant painted image of Ludo's icon Pam and a ladder. Drawn to it irresistibly, Hanna approaches the billboard, and, seeking her son, she climbs up and tries to get into the image, as if, somehow she were actually trying to enter into her child's fantasy world, where he must be, with Pam. Hanna falls from the ladder.

When we see her next, Ludo and the others have gathered around her recumbent form. As she looks up, she reaches for her little son and says:

"You will always be our child. I've tended to forget that recently, but no more."

The last image Berliner offers us is the shimmering figure of Pam, who flies overhead amid frothy clouds and stardust and who, as she vanishes across the screen, bestows a farewell, bewitching, and conspiratorial wink.

The film thus ends on a chord that never fully resolves. *Ma vie en rose* leaves us uncomfortably wondering, yet buoyed by uncertain hope. Could it be that negotiations between children's fantasy lives and the external worlds that surround them both within and outside their families present challenges we would do best to meet with corresponding imaginative inventions of our own? Could it be that mothers may have to climb up ladders into billboards? And even fall off? That they may have to come back from the dead with warm sweaters and loving words for their four year olds? That they may need to lend support to unworldly sons for aching dreams and impractical plans and stand by while their offspring fail but always while envisioning radiant ultimate success? Such moments, such attitudes, are ephemeral but transformative. They are moments that knit the generations together with silken threads of incipient understanding.

Nearly four-year-old Yann is spending the night at his grandparents' home. Earlier he had been shown a DVD of the classic movie version of *The Wizard of Oz* (1939). Trying at nightfall to get him to sleep, his grandparents meet with implacable resistance. The little boy, who has remained terrified of the wicked witch, refuses to close his eyes; he fears the witch will come to get him. Both grandparents work at calming him down and in the process they trot out a battery of well-honed logic and common sense. They muster verbal explanations:

"Witches do *not* exist," they authoritatively proclaim.

This tack, however, proves futile.

They show him that no witches are lurking in the immediate vicinity. The little boy remains fearful. Slowly, they open all the drawers of the dresser. They draw aside the curtains, peer under the bed and the rug. They search the inside of the closet and behind all the clothes hanging there. They even check outside the window. These acts prove equally fruitless. Sitting tensely upright in bed in his pajamas, their small grandson is unmoved by these procedures.

At her wit's end, Yann's grandmother suddenly feels the shock of a lightning bolt! As flashes of inspiration strike, she catches an invisible ball. Disappearing into a nearby bathroom in the hallway, she fills a plastic toothbrush glass with water and brings it back into the room. Triumphantly and dramatically, she presents it to her exhausted but rigidly anxious little grandson who, by this time, is visibly fighting sleep.

"Look, Yann!" she declares. "Here. See this glass of water? I am going to put it right here beside your bed on the night table. If the wicked witch comes, you just pour this right over her!"

And, with that, the little boy finally rests. *Now,* he feels protected and understood; *now,* he can let himself fall off to sleep.

What has happened? How did this grandmother accomplish her goal? I suggest she did so by fully entering, for a crucial moment, her grandson's imaginary world. Realizing that—to *him*—the wicked witch was real, 100 percent, and accepting this premise, she managed to give him exactly what he needed in order to feel safe. She never explained to me quite how she got there, but I am certain it was because she herself could not tell. Everything else had failed. After all, isn't that how it is with life and art: we fail again and again before getting it right. As we saw previously, in the chapter on *Ponette,* as well as here with Ludo, our failures and those of our children have value. They form, when we reflect on them, important elements of understanding.

Picturing Lost Children

Then the mothers were separated from their
children; these were heartbreaking scenes.

—ANNETTE WIEVIORKA

(My translation from the French)

While writing the chapter that follows just after this one, I at-
tended a photography exhibition in Paris at the *Mémorial du
Martyr juif inconnu* (Memorial to the Unknown Jewish Martyr) on the
Île de la Cité and, shortly afterward, I came upon a small book intended for children by the French historian Annette Wieviorka, a spe-
cialist on the Holocaust and the twentieth century in France. Both
Wieviorka's book, *Auschwitz expliqué à ma fille* (Auschwitz Explained to
My Daughter), and the exhibition itself recall to us the helplessness of
parents under conditions of government-sanctioned violence and mass
murder. The parents are, at the same time, implicitly honored. We are
given the wherewithal, even now, so many decades later, to visualize
and cherish—vicariously—their children.

In a basement room, discreetly lit, in the *Mémorial du Martyr juif inconnu* in Paris, I am surrounded by photographs of children. Most of
them were born in the decade of the 1930s. All were French. All were
Jewish. All were seized in the infamous Vél' d'Hiv' roundup by the

Nazis in mid-July of 1942 and deported later that summer, and all were murdered in Auschwitz-Birkenau. Every single child.

I look around me. Each face, body, and expression is unique. Every child is carefully dressed for his or her portrait photograph. Some smile coyly; others seem serious. A tough-looking fellow folds his arms across his chest and glares daringly out at the world. His arrogance reminds me of that Bronzino portrait of a young Florentine nobleman of the early cinquecento I revisited just weeks ago at the Frick Collection in New York. A proud mother offers her two smartly dressed sons to the camera as if, like the ancient Roman matron Cornelia, she wants to say of them, "Look! These are my jewels." A small curly-haired girl in white with patent leather shoes brings to mind snapshots of my younger sister Connie, whose blond ringlets were once the object of my most intense envy. Planted on a bench much too high for her so that her fat legs dangle, her miniature body is balanced by a ceramic pot of flowers no larger than she. Near her, on the wall to the left, a chubby fellow perches perilously on a table covered with a checkered cloth, his fuzzy white toy lamb resting lopsided in his arms. He looks a bit belligerent, as though he might want more than anything else to get down and run around. I can almost tell the lamb was handed to him in exasperation to keep him still.

Beneath him, another mother and her two daughters instantly call to mind a majestic Renoir canvas—that languorous, richly colored portrait in sensuous oils, *Madame Charpentier and Her Children,* which hangs in the Metropolitan Museum of Art—but here, in this photograph, everyone is stiff. The mother and older girl wear, sewn across their hearts, the star that proclaims Juif (Jew). Elegantly dressed in fur-collared pleated coats and matching hats, the girls stand erect beside their mother, whose attire proclaims the height of fashion—hand-stitched leather gloves, a plumed hat, a silk blouse. Even in this formally posed photograph, we can sense the difference between the personalities of the two sisters, the older one more docile and accepting, the younger one independent, rebellious, a trifle fierce, perhaps, and difficult.

Many children hold their favorite toys. I see teddy bears, a very lifelike toy dog, one large rubber ball and several smaller ones, two dollies, a hand puppet, even a miniature violin. One older girl clutches a book tightly held in her left hand and seems almost to be trying to hide it. I feel that nothing would make her put it down. I used to be like that too.

"Why must you always bring a book with you?" my mother would ask in an aggravated tone whenever we went visiting. "It isn't polite, and, besides, there will be no time for you to read it."

But to me, just as to this girl perhaps, the book mattered desperately. I needed to have it. It completed me somehow. Without a book, I could not feel whole.

Another child is nearly dwarfed by the huge white bow that sails her hair. She looks suspicious. Clearly, she does not want to stand there on that pedestal all trussed up, and she is not standing straight. Her eyes seem to demand:

"How long must I endure this? When can I get down? Who are *you*, anyway? I don't like you; so, please just go away!"

A large close-up image portrays a mother with two children who are leaning up against her, all three heads seeming to flow together in the shadow created by their dark hair and the son's hand resting tenderly on his mother's shoulder. The scene conveys a mood of sweetness and serenity unmatched by many of the others, and I am wondering about the love that emanates from all three gazes. Might the photographer himself have been a member of this family, perhaps even woman's husband, the children's father?

Walking slowly over to the next wall, I am confronted by a person stuffed into an enormous padded woolen coat much too big for her. Askew on her legs, her teddy bear reclines, resembling if anything a honey-satiated Pooh. Posed for her portrait on a velvet pillow, this small girl might be taken for a baby doll herself and does not look quite real. On second glance, she reminds me suddenly of my mother, who, as a baby, was endowed with similarly puffy chipmunk cheeks. She, too, was crammed, as she often told us, into layers and layers of woolens, so that eventually, when she went to primary school, the other children teased her and called her a "polar bear." This creature has gaminelike bangs and reaches out toward us with her tiny fists. Young as she is, I think she is definitely posing, and posing, I would wager, for her mother who—just venturing a guess—is standing right beside the photographer.

Finally now, a three-year-old boy named Léon Futerman arrests me. He forces me to stand stock still. It is another close-up: his face looms large. How calmly he looks out at me as we regard one another. I love him already—the steadiness of his gaze and the mischievous curve of his mouth, his look of complete responsiveness to the world. His open curiosity and trust. He has not lost that special look with which new life begins. I can see right away what a wonderful child he is. If I keep standing here, he will break my heart and consume me with the wish to bring him back to life. What might he have grown up to be? This perfectly imperfect little boy. In his picture, he is wearing a white collar over a nubby sweater and crossed straps, which I can imagine fastening for him. One more flick of the hairbrush would make that stray lock fall into place. I am aching to embrace him. Just this one. And *not* to let myself think about what happened to him—and to all the others.

What does an exhibit like this say and do to us? How can we defend ourselves? Another American visitor with a Boston accent walks past me, whispering in denial to her friend:

"But surely not *all* of them could have died . . ."

As for me, sitting here on the floor for hours with my notebook looking up at the faces, gestures, poses, toys, and costumes, unable to leave, my overwhelming impression is that of love. Every one of these children—a small sample of the 4,054 who were rounded up in the Rafle de Vél d'Hiv' and sent to their deaths—was cherished. We can see it on these walls. What happened to them was out of the hands and beyond the ken of those who cared for them. Their fathers and mothers could not protect them. Photographed *en famille* or, when portrayed by themselves, raised up on benches, tables, and elevated platforms, these fresh new lives are presented to us, in this exhibition of photographs, as the precious treasures they once were. And still somehow are.

What matters now, I try to ask myself, if anything matters now? And, returning the gazes of these once noisy children, I think I see that maybe the only way of holding on to them and of holding them is by loving the children of today who, unlike them, are still alive.

But Léon's face makes me doubt that answer. His eyes hold me fast. His straps need a tug. He will not let go of me. He died for nothing. Right? A long time ago. And you and I, we, all of us, know that—as we stand in this room, or imagine it, and as we bring these images back to life with our minds; loving today's children is not an answer unless we believe that one human life can substitute for another.

How hard it is to be here. Yet, harder still to leave. When, finally, I pull myself to my feet to walk away, I am drained. Against the pain in this room, there is no anodyne, no remedy. Against the loss of these bright beginnings, against the forfeiture of this trust, this promise, and this hope, there is no defense. None at all.

Too Young to Understand

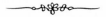

You mustn't ask about that until you are big and grown up.
—HENRIK IBSEN

[in] the no man's land between parents and children
—NAVA SEMEL

What is the purpose of keeping secrets from children? What are the effects? Adults conceal aspects of the past not only for reasons of privacy, prudence, and prudery, but because we want to protect children. We want to prolong their innocence and keep them safe by suppressing what might sully or unsettle them. We hide, therefore, what we deem unsuitable. But we keep silent also because we ourselves cannot brook suffering or an exposure that might cause shame. Something in the past may have stunned or wounded us. Doubtless, we have performed acts of which we cannot feel proud. We may need to flee the reexposure of our well-defended yet vulnerable hearts to former moments of helplessness or humiliation. Why revive them? Moreover, if we refuse to talk about them, maybe they will recede, as per the conceit in Molière's *Tartuffe,* where the impostor—as he tries to seduce Elmire, the beautiful wife of his host—proposes that unless something is talked about it never really takes place. In any case, how *should* we talk about the past? How *can* we explain? Where do we find the right words? Better to remain silent.

Mendel (1997, Norway), directed by Alexander Rosler.
Shown from left: Thomas Jungling Sorensen, Teresa Harder.
(Courtesy of Photofest.)

And what about children's images of us? As heroic? Shall we, like Freud's father, when Sigmund was a boy of twelve, tell stories that might make them lose confidence in us and our ability to protect them? Freud's father said that, once when he was out walking, a Gentile knocked his new fur hat into the gutter and, pejoratively calling him a Jew, ordered him to get off the sidewalk. The shocked child then asked his father how he had responded to the gratuitous insult, but Jakob Freud answered that he simply picked his hat up out of the mud and walked away, an answer that bitterly disappointed Sigmund and rankled for years. What he had wanted to hear from his father was an aggressive retort to the bigot. Thus, blended motives—altruism, self-protection, indolence, and pride—all beguile us into presuming we can and should protect the next generation by covering them each night with a thick blanket of ignorance.

This strategy never works. Curious, sensitive, probing, and irrepressibly ingenious, children, vis-à-vis their concealing parents, are like Dostoyevsky's Porfiry Petrovitch vis-à-vis Raskolnikov in the gripping drama of hide-and-seek that is *Crime and Punishment*. They want and *need* to make sense of what matters to them; they *must* know what happened, and why, and how. Their powerful desire to uncover the truth resists silences that would annul their search and obscure its object. Not right away, not all at once, but eventually. And then, when they find out at last, they feel, not incomprehensibly, betrayed. A bitter question, sometimes left unvoiced, forms and echoes within them: "Why didn't you tell me?"

In the work of artists who have sought to represent this theme, a child's relentless drive to penetrate parental silence may prove both explosive and dangerous. Into gaps made by parents' refusal to talk and by a genuine inability in some cases to do so, avalanches of fantasy, suspicion, misconception, and delusion may fall and burden a child's mind along with other ruinous shards. We must remember, though, that exaggeration in the aesthetic realm serves an important purpose. It enables us to crystallize a problem and bring serious issues into focus. Characters in film and fiction, far from providing us with emulable models, often enact in hypertrophied forms the emotions we occasionally feel but manage under ordinary circumstances to temper, modulate, and deny.

We see all this clearly in a 1997 film made in Norway by Alexander Rosler, a Jew born in postwar Dachau, in 1947. His film, *Mendel*, explores and foregrounds the theme of knowing but not telling. Rosler reveals, little by little, the metastases of malignant symptomatology that proliferate when children are (as one character in the film puts it) "born too late" to have experienced firsthand the brutalities that ravaged their families and deformed their lives. *Mendel* tells its story almost exclusively from the vantage point of the child.

The omission in *Mendel* of any sustained rendering of the parental perspective (as we have seen in the film *Ma vie en rose*) is my strongest critique of the work and has caused me considerable anguish as I have familiarized myself with the literature and artifacts of the period. I have come to feel ever more wary of casting any blame on Bela and Aron, the loving but severely traumatized couple, who fail to explain anything about the past to their younger son. In the following pages, we shall both reflect on these parents, who say almost nothing, and glance at a mother who tries to explain "everything." Both are extremes. By implication, they may teach us to grapple toward compromises that avoid the damaging results of either immoderate solution.

L ilting klezmer music fills our ears as the film begins, and an establishing image takes shape: a tangle of roots, gnarled, broken, and sprawling aboveground, the partially destroyed foundations of a gargantuan unseen tree. Far below, in a valley blurred by distance, one tiny car speeds along. A pale Volkswagen. What comes next zooms in close: a crucified roadside Christ, its carved feet pierced by nails. The first words we hear are those of Mendel Trotzig, the title character, a nine-year-old boy who says in German, "I didn't have any bad memories from Germany." Thus, as in any finely wrought work of art, we have it all with us right from the start.

War, violence, and religious persecution produce noxious psychic matter in all children, but here we are dealing with a child of survivors of the Holocaust, the so-called second generation. As in certain forms of illness, the survivors suffer a poison that has pervaded its victims, wasted them with its toxicity, and, despite occasional respites, pitilessly and relentlessly attacked them from within, inflicting cycles of post-traumatic malfunction that, in a significant number of cases, has led to tragic late life suicide. Even, moreover, when pathology abates and, as in many instances, a measure of health is restored, a permanent cure remains elusive. For the parents of "the second generation," silence in the face of what they witnessed and endured was not a choice. (Just a few of the many distinguished authors who have written about this phenomenon are Dori Laub, Cathy Caruth, Marianne Hirsch, and Saul Friedlander.)

Little Mendel Trotzig has nothing to remember. His opening words are uttered as his family leaves Germany in order to be resettled in Norway in the early 1950s, when the Norwegian government imported a

78

quota of Jews left homeless by the ravages of World War II. Mendel's older brother David, who *does* know what happened in Germany, roughly slams down the window of their compartment on a train several minutes later in the film, thus blocking out the view of what is to him still a terrifying country.

Mendel does not understand. His father, Aron, nervously chain-smokes and compulsively repeats ethnic self-mocking jokes at which other characters titter uneasily. He survived the camps only at the cost of his religious faith, and he now scorns the ritual practices of Judaism. He awakens at night soaked in his pajamas after terrifying dreams. In one recurring oneric episode, his shoes are stolen.

"You can't trust anyone," he tells his little son.

Mendel's mother, Bela, hides photographs. She shoos Mendel away whenever he appears curious. At bedtime, she sings sadly in Yiddish to her older son, David, who softly weeps. Mendel is bewildered by this theater of unintelligible behavior, and his response is to pose a continual stream of questions. Invariably, he is put off with slogans: Be quiet. Go back to bed. You are too young to understand. This is not for children.

Little by little, the family—as a whole and individually—attempts to acclimate itself to its altered life surroundings in Lutheran Norway. Once there, however, it becomes quickly apparent, as can be deduced from the image of the crucified Christ at the start of the film and by a prominent sign in Norwegian—"*Jesus verdens lys*" (Jesus light of the world")—that their kindly hosts have elected to welcome them, not only with the aim of performing charitable deeds but also in order to proselytize and convert them to their own particular form of Christianity. To that end, pious Norwegian characters prepare speeches that sound tactless to this tragic remnant of exiled Jews. They expose the immigrant children of Mendel's cohort to symbols, signs, and songs that seem harmless enough to the children on account of their extreme youth and naïveté but that provoke resentment on the part of the children's survivor parents.

At holiday time, a Norwegian dressed up as Father Christmas offers gifts to the Jewish children. Mendel wants naturally to accept one, but he is admonished by his parents, who see the child's acquiescence as a form of capitulation to religious seduction. They see the gifts as a brazen form of enticement on the part of the Lutherans. During this Christmas party scene, one of the Trotzigs' neighbors, a religious man who is the father of Mendel's friend Markus, remarks pointedly that the goyim may sing tenderly and with feeling about their infant Jesus but, without remorse, they murdered Jewish infants in cold blood. Later in the film, this man's wife repeats this charge with terrible anguish. She asks the pious Lutherans if Jesus can bring her dead children back to life. Mendel looks on. The words make no sense to him. When he asks what they mean, he is rebuffed. He is told to be quiet, and the mantra is intoned that he is too young to understand: what he seeks to know is "not for children."

Unable to speak Norwegian, Mendel, unlike David, is not sent to school right away. In the cramped quarters of the decrepit building in which the family has been lodged after a requisite stay in a welcome shelter, the little boy feels trapped. Lonely and bored, he is ignored by his gentle, disoriented mother who distracts herself by obsessively performing a ceaseless round of domestic chores. The Scandinavian climate proves too severe for daily outdoor play; Mendel is even forbidden to bounce his ball indoors on the stairwells. A bitter, German-hating custodian who lurks about the building with her cleaning implements makes complaints about this activity. Like a tarantula, she materializes spookily to threaten and menace the little boy. Because he and his family are German speakers, she mistakenly assumes they are the enemy and despises them accordingly. Who knows, however, what she herself has suffered? To Mendel, she is a veritable witch or *Hexe*.

Cast into this gloom of paranoia, claustrophobia, and chronic anxiety, the child—in his inchoate way—longs for a return to what he fantasizes as the benign Deutschland they have left behind. Thus, we can see how distortion follows the ignorance perpetrated by parental silence and how it fills gaps when explanations are withheld.

Like Mendel, another child character named Momik (who is not in this film) was created by the Israeli novelist David Grossman (1989) in his work *See Under: LOVE*. I want to mention Momik because he, too, exemplifies this phenomenon. Momik is an Israeli boy of similar age to

Mendel, who likewise struggles fiercely with the secrecy of his elders. Momik tries with every fiber of his being to decipher the meaning of what happened "Over There," in other words, in the European theater of war and death during World War II.

Returning to Rosler's film, on the eve of Yom Kippur, the most solemn day of the Jewish year, Mendel watches his religious neighbor lay tefillen (as he prepares to pray), and he notices, on the man's bare arm, a row of numbers stamped into the flesh. Mendel stares at these marks, and, as he does so, the unhappy child surmises that they must have come from Germany along with the man himself. Therefore, he asks wistfully:

"Can I have a number like that too?"

Needless to say, this innocent request meets with chilled horror on the part of his parents. Mendel is left once again with no understanding. Later on, in imitation of these "desirable" marks from Germany, he actually paints a set of numbers on his friend Markus's arm, an act that scandalizes all the adults in both families. Yet, even now, the mortified parents provide no explanation for their reaction and no guidance. The children remain ignorant. They learn nothing except that they have angered their parents.

In an analogous scene, in Grossman's novel, the little Israeli Momik, who gives daily care to his deranged survivor uncle, whom he calls "Grandfather" because his real grandfather is no longer alive, tries to wash the concentration camp numbers off the old man's arm with soap, water, and spit. Momik rubs and scrubs with all his might, but to no avail. Once he realizes that he cannot succeed, he reflects that, whereas dirt or ink, which come to the body's surface from the outside, *can* be removed by this method but these numbers cannot, he begins to imagine that there must be some mystery about them. Puzzled and fascinated, Momik fantasizes about what the numbers are and where they might have come from. Could they have arisen somehow from *inside* Grandfather? And what could they mean? Momik guesses that the numbers have letter equivalencies, as in *gematria,* a system in which the Hebrew alphabet is associated with meanings and numbers in the kabbalah. Perhaps, he ponders, the numbers on the old man's arm possess some arcane, spiritual, or magic significance. He speculates whether, like the secret numerical combinations used to open a safe, they could, if deciphered, make his grandfather split apart so that, instead of the demented old man he is, a saner, healthier, more responsive grandfather might emerge. Thus little Momik carries on various experiments, trying with all his might to understand. When his efforts fail, he feels "strangely sad." As Grossman knowingly writes, he goes over to embrace his grandfather tenderly and hug him tight. The numbers will not yield. Not even to love.

Let's return to the film. Mendel, in a state of mingled frustration, apathy, ennui, and pent-up energy, needs to escape from the strictures of his caring but resolutely unresponsive family. He wanders off and climbs the stairs of the building where his family's apartment is located. Passing hanging items of laundry and exposed wires, he reaches the uppermost level under the eaves. There, to his surprise, he comes upon a solitary human being—an old man, a Norwegian, who seems to be living all by himself in a small open area with a humble pallet and a few rudimentary supplies. This unexpected apparition seems uncanny to Mendel, who observes him stealthily from a safe distance in the attic half-light. He notices that the man is absorbed in carving a small horse out of wood. Mesmerized, standing perfectly still, the little boy watches from his post, while the old man, who seems reminiscent of Ibsen's character Ekdal from *The Wild Duck* (1884)—similarly an aged attic denizen—becomes aware of his presence. Neither speaks. Some magnetic force draws the boy in closer, and, finally, the old man comments that it is good to have a place of one's own where one can have peace.

With that, he reaches out and hands Mendel a block of wood and a piece of sandpaper. This simple gesture is exactly what our lonely, displaced child needs. The wise stranger has performed an act of empathy. In one fell swoop, he has fulfilled two of Mendel's most pressing lacks. He has offered the boy a real task to perform, a manageable one with a clear goal and thus a way to feel useful rather than superfluous. And he has included Mendel in his own endeavors rather than shunting him aside as everyone else does. Immediately, Mendel begins to work on sanding his block. After this fortuitous encounter, he mounts the stairs regularly and spends time with the old man in the attic.

Soon we learn that a young woman, apparently a grown daughter, visits Mendel's new friend on a regular basis with her baby in her arms; it is she who delivers his meals and administers his basic care. Mendel witnesses the old man's pleasure when she appears and he can fondle his grandchild, her plump baby. In a natural, gracious way, whenever Mendel is present, the old man offers him a portion of his food to share, and Mendel—with a growing boy's voracious appetite—partakes willingly, consuming with relish helpings of cold potatoes and herring. By watching, helping, and quietly communing, the immigrant child finds solace with this native stranger, and it is clear that the visits afford them both a mutual satisfaction.

Downstairs with his family, however, Mendel worries about his *own* grandparents. Where, he wants to know, is *his* grandfather? Why does no one speak of him? He poses this question outright, but his parents give no answer. Mendel persists. He points out the discrepancy that, whereas grandfathers *do* exist here in Norway, he, Mendel, has none. Pressed, his mother finally responds by offering him a partial truth:

"Our old ones were the first to die," she says cryptically.

Her statement, devoid of any modifying context, makes, as usual, no sense to Mendel. It fails to clarify or resolve his problem. He knows, after all, that there was war in Norway, too; yet, in Norway, there are, nonetheless, grandparents. Throwing her hands up, his mother finally, in desperation, silences him and pronounces her dictum that he is not yet old enough to understand.

At last, one day, the old man finishes his carving, and he hands his wooden horse to Mendel. Thrilled with the gift, all the more precious because so spontaneously and unexpectedly given and because it is an object whose genesis and evolution he has witnessed, Mendel accepts it, and, in a gesture that mirrors the apparent impetuousness of its bestowal, he jumps into the old man's arms and embraces him with the unique fervor of a truly happy child. Delicately holding his treasure, Mendel brings it downstairs and plays with it in his family's apartment.

He shows it off proudly to them, but when they ask him where he got it, he slyly turns the tables on them and announces triumphantly that *this* is *his* secret!

His survivor parents cannot play games. Insecure and mistrustful, they cannot—despite their own concealments—fathom the levels of meaning in Mendel's joke. Instead of learning from it, or honoring it, they simply grow fearful. They will not permit Mendel to have any secrets from them. They question him until he gives in and reveals the truth about his visits to the elderly Norwegian grandfather who lives upstairs in solitude.

This revelation prompts a volley of vituperation, which erupts and crescendos from the mouths of both parents. Stricken with horror at their son's hidden friendship with a person who, in their minds, may prove a sinister foreigner, a goy, they verbally chastise Mendel. They deny him all further access to the old man and forbid him to go upstairs in the future. They forbid him to accept gifts from persons unknown to the family. Hearing this, we hark back to the Christmas scene earlier in the film and to the parents' concerns that all gifts to Jewish children from non-Jews may prove a means of seduction and persuasion, a design to lure them away from their gnarled roots.

Parenthetically, it may be worth recalling here that, among the most repugnant anti-Semitic Nazi picture books of the prewar era made for German children and distributed by the propagandistic Stürmer Verlag of Nuremberg, a similar message was given in reverse. One such book, *Der Giftpilz* (The Poisoned Mushroom) of 1934, features among its illustrations an obese, unshaven, bulbous-nosed Jew offering bags of sweets in the street to blonde, blue-eyed "Aryan" children. Thus, bigotry and fear recrudesce, betraying the xenophobia that motivates them. In such moments, we confront our own irrational, overwrought suspicion and mistrust of those who appear different from ourselves.

Mendel protests until finally his father, in an outburst of rage, grabs the little wooden horse and hurls it to the ground, thus breaking off one of its legs. Startled by this violent act, the boy cringes. His parents' behavior, as always, baffles him and fails to enlighten him. This time it appears as cruel as it is unreasonable. We, on the other hand, watching the story unfold onscreen, can assume a distance unavailable to the characters. We can sense the invisible terror that pervades Bela and Aron. We can recognize the cracked lenses through which they must filter Mendel's surreptitious forays into the attic. Unlike them, locked as they are into their respective viewpoints, we, watching, can sympathize both with the child's pain at his loss and with the wellsprings of fear that motivate his exiled parents.

With power and clarity, the film goes on in this way to portray the fallout of adult secrecy. Wishing to keep Mendel innocent of the Holocaust, his mother and father cannot step back to consider that being in the dark does not lead to a child's peace of mind. "Not telling," we are made to see, places its own inescapable burden on the one who is not told and its own heavy load of anxiety. At the milder end of the spectrum, Mendel is simply confused and bewildered. The inscrutability of his parents' reactions to daily life makes it hard for him to feel at ease in the new world that surrounds him. At the more extreme end of the spectrum, he gradually starts to exhibit acute symptoms, symptoms, however, that bespeak the fact that, notwithstanding their occasional severity, Mendel is a child who knows he is securely loved. In this sense, he reminds us both of Ponette and Ludovic Fabre. His parents are normally affectionate and kind.

Like Ponette, who loses her mother in a car accident, Mendel evinces resiliency and an adaptive strength that carry him through. Never capitulating to the unnamed malaise that lurks below the surface of his parents' silence, he pushes back. Unlike Momik in Grossman's novel, he never grows thin and pale from anxiety. He possesses an innate toughness, a capacity to act and react, and, because of the felt presence of his parents' love, no matter how ill-expressed at times, he does not crumble into passivity. Like Ponette, and unlike Momik, he prevails, at least to some extent, in his struggle against censorship and concealment. This comes, however, at a cost we cannot measure.

Meanwhile, pictures in his mind join and overlap in bizarre formations so that, like his father Aron, Mendel soon begins to awaken at night with bad dreams. He loses urinary control from time to time, and these disturbances—of sleep and bladder—seem blatantly symptomatic of his chronic failure to exert control over his life cognitively. Snooping among his mother's private articles, he casts about like a detective for the photographs she has sequestered, and, when he finds an album, he searches it for pictures of his missing grandparents.

At one point, while secretly paging through, he notices empty spaces, and he surmises that photos of people who died must have occupied these spaces. In an effort to be helpful and honor these dead relations, he takes a pen and marks black crosses on every page where a space denotes that a photograph was removed. He does this as a child growing up in Norway who, by this time, six months later, attends a local school. He has learned that crosses are the conventional way Norwegians commemorate their dead in graveyards as well as in newspapers. Coming into the room as he is performing this innocent act while, in his mother's eyes, defiling the family album with black crosses, Bela is beside herself. Snatching the book away, she protests:

"We are not Christians," she tells him: "We are Jews."

Once again, the sentence means little to Mendel who, shortly afterward, is shown sitting in school while a sanctimonious female teacher weeps in front of the children as she tells them, slowly and deliberately—and with full awareness of Mendel's presence—the poisonous story of how the Jews allowed Jesus to die by choosing to free Barabbas instead: "The Jews killed Jesus." We cannot tell whether Mendel makes any connection between his teacher's story and his mother's horror at the crosses in the family album. Such unprocessed, uninterpreted, disconnected experiences, however, along with other fragments, including scenes from a fire that actually takes place in their building one night, as well as fantasies about the war in Germany, which occurred before he could remember it, his father's recurrent nightmares, and images of the forbidden old man in the attic—all merge in his mind to produce nightmares and bed-wetting.

On Yom Kippur, we experience one of the most wrenching scenes of the film. It is so affecting because here we enter momentarily into a parent's perspective as well as a child's. Spurning religion, Mendel's father Aron has insisted on eating and behaving as usual during this holy day of fasting and remembrance. By contrast, Markus's family next door is observing the holy day normally with abstinence and prayer. Watching them and wanting to imitate them, Mendel puts on a hat and shawl; he is eager to participate in their rituals. Aron grows angry at this and shouts at the little boy. Markus's father now opens the door between the two apartments and softly admonishes Aron for chastising his son on such a holy day and for showing disrespect to the dead.

Bela turns pale. Disappearing into another room where she covers her head with a lace veil, she prepares to light candles. The boys gather near her, and we hear soft chanting coming from next door. Aron paces up and down the room, smoking. Suddenly, he strides over to the grandfather clock against the wall and begins to strike his forehead repetitively with his fist, a movement that shifts so that soon he is striking his forehead itself against the hard surface of the clock. Each time he hits himself, he speaks a name and repeats it: "Benjamin, Elias, Benjamin." Watching this in horror, little Mendel runs to him begging:

"Papa, stop!" he pleads, "I'll never wear a hat again."

Rather than turn timid, self-conscious, and pathologically antisocial, as some children would and as many did (including the fictional Momik), Mendel veers in the opposite direction. Six months later, the family relocates to the countryside. Mendel befriends a group of blonde Norwegian children who attend his neighborhood school, and, in their company, he grows increasingly brash and reckless. Experiencing himself as other than the passive, helpless victim he confusedly associates with being "a Jew," he eventually performs a dangerous act of aggression that, fortunately, miscarries. He attempts, using live ammunition, to shoot a gun he has learned to handle, having been instructed by a local farmer, the father of one of his new friends at school, to kill someone.

The target of Mendel's misguided aggression is a masked man who gallops by on the road every day in a horse-drawn cart. Dark gloves cover this stranger's hands, he never speaks, and he cracks his whip over the back of his horse. Mendel's friends refer to him as "the Mitten-Man," and they invent wild fantasies about him. They speculate on the origins of his supposedly hideous deformities. They repeat descriptions of his alleged lewdness, depravity, and salacious practices. With childish naïveté, Mendel decides that he will become a hero by doing away with this fellow who, he concludes, must surely be an "anti-Semite." Not clear, however, what this term means, Mendel prays:

"Dear God, Buddha, Allah, Jesus, let me meet a real anti-Semite so I can fight back."

His appeal reminds us of Ponette who, longing for her mother's return, similarly invokes every deity she can think of so as to hedge her bets.

Mendel aims the farmer's gun, one day, at the so-called Mitten-Man as the fellow rides by, and shoots. When the stranger's horse shies and rears, Mendel falls to the ground. In profound shock, the startled driver halts. Outraged that the boy has threatened him this way, he takes off his mask and points out furiously that his horse might have been injured or killed. Mendel claims responsibility. He announces that he is a Jew. The man responds by pointing out, both to Mendel and to the other children (who have timorously crept back after scattering and have reappeared now to watch what happens) that, in fact, *they have no idea who he is.*

"Do you know who I am?" he asks them angrily. And then, he says with feeling:

"Maybe I am a Jew, too, or a gypsy."

To this, there can be only silence.

Thus, the film raises questions about the conditions for learning about matters that are all but impossible to teach. As adults, we have, in fact, no answers to the hardest questions children broach. Even if adults would and could talk, how might they give satisfaction? In David Grossman's novel, a time comes when little Momik begins to go to the library to read about what happened "Over There." He attempts *The Diary of Anne Frank* and other books but finds he cannot understand much of what he is encountering there. He appeals to his family's kindly neighbor, Bella Marcus, who tries to respond to his questions. He asks her about "the death train" and why they killed small children and about how people feel when they have to dig their own graves and whether Hitler had a mother and whether they really made soap out of human bodies and what it means to make experiments on human beings?

We never learn Bella's answers. Momik, however, grows increasingly worried and distraught. As his mental state and physical condition deteriorate, Bella stops answering him. By this time, he has secretly caught and caged several small animals in the cellar of the building where he lives because he has conceived the bizarre idea that, through them, he can somehow vanquish the terrible "Nazi Beast," which he thinks of in literal terms; hence, the live animals. To bait, coax, trick, and foil this so-called Nazi Beast, Momik cuts yellow stars out of cardboard and glues them to his father's old overcoat, which he dons in the basement. He covers his arms with numbers from discarded lottery tickets. Disguised this way so as to impersonate what he conceives of as "the Jew," he sits motionless for hours in the dark after school with the caged animals, waiting (like Ponette for her dead mother) for the Nazi Beast to appear. In unconscious imitation of the secrets that circulate in the air he breathes, Momik tells no one of these occult activities. Meanwhile, Bella notices his pallor and sees that he has grown thinner and more abstracted and estranged with each passing day. She feels terribly guilty. She is overcome with remorse; she believes that, by trying to answer his questions, she has harmed him and driven him insane.

What, after all, we wonder, as we reflect on these scenes, *can* children gain from adult answers and explanations? Especially when we try to explain to them what is beyond our own comprehension.

One day in Paris, I came upon a small book entitled *Auschwitz expliqué à ma fille* (Auschwitz Explained to My Daughter) by the French historian Annette Wieviorka (1999). Curious, I found in it a well-crafted dialogue between the author and her daughter, Mathilde, in which the daughter's questions (about what actually took place regarding the Jews during the war) are clearly and accurately answered by her highly knowledgeable mother. Initially, I deemed the book a model. It reminded me of a statement by the distinguished American psychologist and educator Jerome Bruner, who wrote, "There is no reason to believe that any subject cannot be taught to any child at virtually any age in some form" ([1960] 2003, 47). Wieviorka, in this modest French text, apparently exemplified that audacious claim.

Yet, as I reread the book more closely, my assessment changed. This is because we hear in it only one voice; we hear the calm rational sentences of the historian mother as she reveals the most inhuman facts of the Holocaust to her child and does not palliate its painful details. In response to each of her statements, the "child," like a mechanical puppet, poses a follow-up question. Indeed, there is no child in the book. There is an automaton with a child's name, a robotic question-generating puppet. Given that the author has adopted a dialogic structure for rhetorical purposes and that the book only pretends to be a realistic representation of an actual parent-child interaction, it nonetheless falls short. It betrays the conceit of a Socratic dialogue, for the original Socratic dialogues, in addition to their logical step-by-step inquiry, expressed an important vein of *feeling*.

In this case, we find an impassive child character who—hearing, from her own mother's lips, sentences about what was perpetrated on women and small children—fails to evince any emotion. Is there a child alive who would simply move on to pose the next question? Yet, surely, a child's emotional response to what she is hearing from her mother needs to be an integral part of such a text. *The reason for this is that the child's emotional reaction is itself a crucial part of the story that needs to be passed on.* It should never be blanched out. Without it, the project rings hollow.

I would go further. Insofar as a parent-child dialogue such as this is sanitized and purged of feeling, it uncannily repeats—*in this sense*—a species of "cleansing." Children who learn about the Holocaust in terms of statistics and gruesome facts tend to treat this history as if it were a fictional horror story. Or, just as they memorize baseball statistics—the number of home runs and so on—they learn to recount the number of victims gassed or Jewish soap bars. They comprehend nothing. Thus, the "dialogue," with its dispassionate rendition and dry tone, fosters distortion. I prefer richly honest, imaginative works of art for children such as, for example, *Rose Blanche,* by Christophe Gallaz and Roberto Innocenti (1985), a picture book in which a non-Jewish girl compassionately takes risks to help Jewish victims behind barbed wire but is then shot in turn by the liberators, so that the book offers no answers but only sadness and unending questions.

Children, Bruner teaches us, *can* grasp some part of difficult truths provided that what is offered to them matches and builds on their present level of understanding. In Wieviorka's case, her daughter Mathilde is meant to be thirteen and thus capable of formal operational thought in a Piagetian sense. In other words, she could be expected to be able to grasp potential relationships and hypotheticals, which would not be the case with our fictional Mendel and Momik who, because they are younger, are still operating quite literally and concretely. Mathilde, moreover, would be farther removed historically from the Holocaust than either of the boys; her mother, born in 1948, would be of Mendel's and Momik's own generation. Yet this fact should have little bearing on a child's capacity to be moved by what happened.

To accept Bruner's premise, as I do, is to locate the problem of secrecy and silence not in children's own supposed inability to comprehend but in adults' incapacity to tell. But adults affected by trauma, like those portrayed by Rosler and Grossman, may well be incapable of telling. As victims of split consciousness, having endured torture, shame, confusion, and far worse, how can they find the words to tell? Neither Grossman, within his literary genre, nor Rosler, in his visual format of film, probes the situation with respect to his own respective set of parent characters.

Notwithstanding this, both works of art remind us that being a parent calls for more than affection and care. Being a parent demands uneasy efforts at learning and teaching. It calls for awkward, halting efforts to share with our children what we have suffered, what has happened and not happened, what might have happened, what may happen, and what we hope will or will never happen. It calls for attention to *their* silences. It calls for valiant forays, whenever possible, into "the no-man's land between parents and children," a phrase coined by the Israeli writer, Nava Semel. Semel's novel, *And the Rat Laughed* (2008), recounts the story of a small Jewish girl who, during the war "Over There," is given by her doomed parents to farmers who hide her in an underground pit with a rat. The story comes to light for the first time only when the girl has become old enough to share it finally with a beloved granddaughter. Children, as we have seen, when they are not told, try to find out for themselves. For Mendel, as for Momik, the learning often comes at great risk.

Returning now to the film, it is not—in the end—Mendel's parents but his older brother David who helps him learn and face some of the unbearable truths of the Holocaust. This happens in a way that involves several moments of abject horror for both boys, and I want to underline the point that it is the absence of parental guidance that propels the sibling intervention. I am about to describe a scene that involves no parental figures onscreen but includes them implicitly. Their incapacity to teach Mendel what he needs causes a penultimate confrontation between the two brothers.

In the vacuum created by Mendel's traumatized parents, the following scene occurs. Playing daily with his Norwegian friends after the resettlement, Mendel hears boasts and tales of *their* fathers' bravery against the Germans during the war. He finds photographs that depict emaciated Jews in prison garb in the camps with hostile German guards watching. He knows that none of his own grandparents is alive. He has been told he is a Jew but grasps almost nothing about what that means and still less about what actually happened to Jews during the war and why *they* did not have guns, like the Germans, or fight back bravely, as did the Norwegians, or so he thinks.

One afternoon, while David is studying at his desk presumably doing homework, Mendel comes in and barrages him with his usual list of questions.

"Why don't you tell me about the war?" the younger boy asks. Why (he wants to know) weren't the Jews brave? Why didn't they resist? Why didn't they snatch the guns from their enemies' hands and fight back? Why? Nobody is ever going to be allowed to do that to me! Why did they stand around like sheep? They just prayed.

Disturbing as these questions are and motivated persuasively by Mendel's contact with the contrasting stories of his new Norwegian friends, there may be a suspicion when we hear them uttered by this child character onscreen that they have been planted there by the filmmaker, Rosler, who is putting into Mendel's mouth a familiar militaristic ideology espoused by the Israeli Zionists, whose aggression was and is fueled by the heartfelt cry "Never again." If so, however, the imposition is not gratuitous. It makes psychological sense. For the etiology of such feelings, both for the child and for the adult political ideologue, remains the same. In any case, Mendel repeats it all and mimics the davening (swaying) motions of a pious Jew at prayer while insolently making the sound "Baaa-aaa."

"Why didn't they do something?" he asks again. He, Mendel, would not have been so cowardly. He would have grabbed a gun from the firing squad and died resisting bravely.

David squirms at his desk. He tries gallantly to shoo his little brother away and continue studying. He makes several efforts to deflect Mendel's onslaught.

"You haven't experienced anything," he tells him: "You were born too late to die."

Mendel, who does not understand this, persists in his davening and sheep imitation.

Finally, exasperated beyond his adolescent, far from perfect self-control, David rises silently from his chair. Infuriated now by Mendel's taunts, he attacks his brother. He pins Mendel to the ground. Once again, there is no clarification. Holding him down and breathing heavily with exertion and emotion, David demands an apology. Mendel, however, who still understands nothing about the Holocaust, insolently repeats his "Baa-aaaa."

At this point, David loses his composure entirely. He picks Mendel up, and, with a flash of sadistic inspiration, he commences a brutal moment of instruction. He takes his struggling younger brother to the open window of the apartment. They are several stories up in the building with the ground far below. Holding the boy by his ankles so that he is upside down outside the high window, David demands:

"Say you're sorry or I'll let you go."

Mendel shakes his head, and we watch in horrified fascination as David shakes him by his feet over the window ledge and warns:

"This is no game, you little Satan."

Finally, Mendel murmurs "Mercy," and David pulls him back inside. Standing him on the floor, he looks down at him and says, contemptuously, that he had his chance but his pride ran out.

Both boys notice that Mendel has wet his pants from fear.

There is no need to point to a moral, no need to say that no one has the right to predict his own bravery in the face of death. Mendel, after his brother's lesson, seems chastened and momentarily subdued. But he is unvanquished and still just as ignorant about what happened in Germany as he was before. He swerves and runs away from his brother. He dashes into the bathroom, where he locks the door defiantly.

In a split-frame screen, we see the faces of both brothers on either side of the door. Mendel opens it just a crack, and, at that, David instantly grabs him and squeezes him into a second deadly headlock. As Mendel winces, we watch, horrified. But very slowly, this time, the aggression melts into an embrace. The two brothers hug each other, and David, with genuine affection, admits:

"You're awfully irritating, but you're brave."

"Then," begs Mendel, "Tell me . . ."

Only now, after learning with life and limb at stake that no one can stand in the place of another, the boys finally begin to talk. For the first time, truths about the war are spoken. Secrets are shared. The Shoah and the concealed photographs are openly discussed. As they are, David reveals to Mendel that his birth father died in Germany while resisting the Nazis and that Aron is, therefore, Mendel's own true father but not his. Past and present finally begin to clarify and make some kind of sense. Puzzle pieces start fitting together, and blurred shapes come forward gradually into sharper focus. Images that were superimposed slowly separate and therefore become intelligible.

At the very end of the film, we watch Mendel perform an act of derring-do. He climbs a rickety ladder set to a dizzying height against the apartment building, his mother watching askance from the window, and, with an umbrella in his hand, he jumps down to the grass below in slow motion while his family, friends, and neighbors stand by, and he lands, at last, safely. We realize in this final scene of mingled fantasy and reality that the child's entire way of being in the world, his personality itself, his recurring needs to reexpose himself to danger and master it, have been molded by what we have witnessed—by the pulling down of shades on the train from Germany, by the sequestering of photographs, by the smashing of the little wooden horse, by the ankle hold outside an open window, and by the perpetual refrain "You are too young to understand."

Reflecting on the film, we may doubt that, whereas it may have seemed clear initially that breaking through silence, divulging secrets, and answering a child's questions on a level best suited to his or her cognitive development would constitute the best strategy, this viewpoint is entirely convincing. After living through the art, we may find ourselves reluctant to subscribe to a doctrine that advocates for the supervalent efficacy of adult verbal explanations. We might return once again to Ponette and her confusing conversations with her well-meaning aunt, her father, her teacher, her peers; to her experiments—inside the garbage can, for instance; to her make-believe shooting on the playground. We might turn back to Mendel's drawings of numbers and crosses and to David's terrible, inexorable lesson, which was physical and dangerous. Each stressful sequence of trial and error occurs and fails before the words that are finally spoken can make sense to the respective child. In both films, the protagonists, "too young to understand," undergo a process of coconstructing meaning with others and for themselves across a variety of experiential modalities. In the end, some of what the parents have kept silent remains so. The children learn what *they* need to learn, and this is always something different.

In the mind of David Grossman's Momik—unlike Mendel—there is a downward spiral. Words float like flakes of confetti in the air he breathes; chameleonlike, they morph into signifiers whose referents come unraveled from public discourse. Spinning off toward meanings of their own, they enmesh this child in a maze of whirling, disjointed, undecipherable signs. The harder he tries to understand, the more isolated he becomes until, ultimately, his world devolves uncannily into a veritable simulacrum of "Over There." In fantasy, in darkness, Momik reenacts the unassimilated trauma from which his family has suffered—the unpredictable chaos and loss of meaning in the camps. He is, at last, sent away from home to recover.

Because each child, parent, and situation differs, we have no formula to help us find a way to forestall the obliteration of what matters. Yet what matters must be communicated and passed on. Moreover, what matters *will,* in some form, be passed on. Even in defiance of all the taboos. Children find out: something. No one is too young to understand.

As to shaping and saving, how much are we up for? To live briefly with Mendel and again with Momik is to be sure there is no right way and no avoidance of risk. Conscious secrets and silences can, on the part of parents, even constitute a species of truth. For a while. They can be nonexpedient and respectful, as Ibsen tries to show us in an earlier Norwegian setting, that is, in his tragic play *The Wild Duck.* We learn this, there, through the protective secrets of a character called Gina Ekdal, who is the mother of a daughter who—as another character suddenly reveals—may be and probably is illegitimate. We are asked to confront the fact that truth alone can never constitute the highest value in human affairs. Ibsen shows us that little Hedvig, Gina's daughter, loses her father's love as soon as the uncertainty of his paternity is made known. Coldly, this father rejects his formerly beloved child because she no longer seems to belong to him and because he assumes that his wife, whom he associates with her, has betrayed him. Hedvig understands nothing except that her adored father has abandoned her. Stealthily, she takes her grandfather's pistol, climbs up into the attic, and shoots herself.

Silence, ultimately, proves lethal. With or without words, we must keep some lines of communication open. Mutism and parental withdrawal into abysses of self beget the annihilation of children. Hedvig's father forsakes her, Momik's parents retreat behind the sealed confines of their lottery booth, Mendel's parents—mum and fearful—stand by.

Children need what may best be conveyed only piecemeal. In fragments. By means of zigzags, with stops, coughs, clumsy interruptions, and by means of approximations. With awkward gestures, reenactments, blurred imagery, by displacement and metaphor. They need chances to be together with us in ways that foster the cocreation of mutual understanding on whatever levels that understanding can take place over time. We see this at the end of *Ponette* in the fantasy scene in which the little girl's dead mother reappears and plays with her. Such methods may work well for us too. Perhaps this is why we crave the arts. What matters needs to be retold a hundred times in myriad ways. With kisses, and with flowing tears, or with blank and stony faces, with hand-carved wooden horses, or with dry eyes that no longer have the wherewithal to weep.

Pinches and Kisses

———◦·᪄ᵻ᪄·◦———

> We looked at each other, and I could see the frightening
> black thing leave her to meet the frightening black thing that
> had left me. They met in the middle and embraced.
>
> —JAMAICA KINCAID

Mothers and daughters choreograph dances that open and close the spaces between them. They perform for one another on stages partly hidden from the world. No one beyond the curtain catches more than a glimpse of their pirouettes. No one knows for certain whether they are embracing or bedeviling each other in confidential pas de deux that persist beyond the grave. No one sees them clearly as they reach, *balancer,* spot and whirl, drop down, contract, spring forward, twist, and repeat. Yet, clear-eyed and unsparing, Jamaica Kincaid unveils these dances in her 1983 novel *Annie John.* Snapping back the curtain, she exposes a daughter and mother who, with mounting guile and suspicion, perform duets propelled by an inexorable force both magnetic and expulsive. Spellbound, we watch them glide blissfully in unison then fall bitterly from intimacy into estrangement.

Unlike the previous chapters, which dealt with painting, photography, and film, we turn here to a novel. Words morph into images as we read. John Updike once, with reference to the magical prose of Bruno Schulz, described the novel as that "great transmogrifier of the world into words." To be astounded by this taken-for-granted phenomenon, we have only to spend a few hours with a child who is learning to read. Not an idle aperçu, for those hours coax back the wonder that lies dormant in us. What a loss that we have ceased to marvel at the sorcery of coded signs on paper and how amazing it is that they give us access to optical experiences as vivid as luminously colored moving pictures. It is in childhood that we first become aware of this property of written texts and how, with the collaboration of our imagination, they bloom into florid visuality. This is why children read with full corporeal absorption and hate to be interrupted.

Such *verbal visuality*, if we may call it that, abounds in the pages of Jamaica Kincaid's coming of age novel *Annie John*. Set on the Caribbean island of Antigua, its sensuousness and gripping intensity make it indispensable to our study of art's wisdom. It takes us right into the core of childhood. It does so, however, by means of words that serve like spades or trowels, for Kincaid's words dig into the soil of the heart and toss it all, dense, moist, granular, clodded, and clumped, into our stinging eyes. We flinch, cowering at what she has cast: a fused, intimate, idealized portrait of a mother-child bond that shatters. Not because of outside forces but because of forces operating within the couple itself. Sweetness spoils, tenderness curdles, trust goes bad. We wince and blink as we read. But, while we are blinking, we begin to notice something else. Little by little, rubbing our eyes, we begin to see that what is most deeply embedded in this story cannot be beheld with eyes wide open. For it is a secret and one not even known to the characters themselves. This secret is that *nothing*—not silence, not lies, not physical distance, nor even death itself—can sever the primal bond. With finality. No matter how far apart the couple grows, the attachment, in some unforeseeable form, perdures. As one of my own daughters explained, it is like celery cord. Tough, elastic, resilient, indestructible, it holds even after the stalk itself has been sliced through.

Kincaid's story might even be read as a modern midrash on the Demeter-Persephone myth (as told by Hesiod and Ovid) but in the daughter's, not the mother's, voice.

Both as literary masterpiece and as psychological diamond mine,

Annie John demands we see it in its glittering verbal visuality. Its phastasmic images take shape in our mind's eye as we read: motifs emerge and zoom into focus—a wooden trunk all filled with memories, painted yellow and green and lined with roseate wallpaper; a mother's alien hands that have held, touched, and bathed a dead girl; a cache of forbidden marbles that is guarded by a daughter from her mother with arrant lies; a snake slithering out of a basket of figs on a mother's head; the perfumed waters of languid mother-daughter baths and the limitless waters of their surrounding cerulean tropical sea; a bevy of girls gathering in a graveyard after school to whisper secrets while showing off their body parts to one another; and a dyad of girls who meet on a hill to pinch and kiss and cry out from their exquisitely fleeting, self-induced thrills. Through images such as these a refracted light illumines the text and showers it with drama, scattering a stardust of reflections and associative meanings that shimmer for us as we bring them into the purview of our own more pallid lives.

Narrated in the first person, *Annie John* is told in the voice of a girl who has been given the same name as her mother. How strange this seems at first and yet on second thought not strange at all but eerily just. For well we might ask whether there is not a sense in which *every* daughter has the same name as her mother: the same shape, the same body, the same developmental path, even though, superficially, it would seem otherwise. Is this not the fundamental twinning that forms a girl's sexual identity and, at the same time, her powerful need to break away? Precisely how old Annie is meant to be when she looks back on her life to tell us her story we do not know, but what we do know quite soon is that she unearths the underbelly of growing up, the parts concealed by reticence, convention, and shame. Boldly, as daughter and mother both, Kincaid retrieves in this book the detritus of maturation, the refuse we consign to oblivion, the abject elements we repress. Trembling at her truths even when the childhoods we remember lend inadequate testimony to the anguish they unveil, we follow her at a discreet distance but not so much as to lose sight of her. For, as with every artist worthy of the name, she has risked a necessary descent, queasy and unlit, into the abysses of herself and she dares us to take the risk of venturing there with her.

Her descriptive powers include, moreover, not only scenes of anguish but of zestful humor as in the deft sketches she makes of Annie's teachers seen through the girl's eyes. One, for example, called Miss Moore, "looked like a prune left out of its jar a long time" and "sounded as if she had borrowed her voice from an owl." This person's throat "beat up and down as if a fish fresh out of water were caught inside." Another teacher, Miss Edward, had eyes that bulged out of her head so that "I was sure that at any minute they would land at my feet and roll away." This person, when she moved about the classroom, passed among the students "like an eclipse."

Such word-pictures beam us back to our own childhoods and children's endless fascination with the uncanny oddities of adult (and especially of parental) bodies. To me, they bring back a pillowy personage of hefty corpulence who taught singing in our New York elementary school. I cannot recall her name or face. Her arms, however—as she raised them to lead us in song—will forever evoke in me a quiver of recognition. Perhaps to avoid becoming overheated, she wore, no matter what the season, a variety of sleeveless or short-sleeved blouses; thus, her pendulous underarms were perpetually on view. Like gelatinous waves, they billowed as she conducted our glee club. Standing on a riser among the second sopranos, I stared awestruck at those undulating mounds of flesh, mesmerized by them as I sang. Obsessively, I wondered how it would feel to possess such arms and what they would be like to touch. They seemed so soft and yielding. And what about our parents' bodies? Which were, of course—at least for some of us—strenuously forbidden, taboo.

Between the age of ten, when her story starts, and seventeen, when it stops, Annie reanimates the demise of her childhood. She has no interest in being evenhanded about it: we gain no access whatever to the inner workings of her mother's psyche. Here we march straight into the young girl's heart as she shadows her mother. We inhabit her world and stay with her for nearly a decade. We swing with her changing

moods and perceptions and within the shifting dimensions of her developing body—the sudden spurts of growth, the elongating bones,
the hair sprouting in new places, the unanticipated bodily smells and
sensations. We are made to feel how dramatic and frightening this all is
—these growing years, this puberty—with its edge of raw dread that we,
thankfully, have effaced from memory. To underscore its terror, Kincaid uses *new* ten times in one paragraph and then seven times again in
quick succession. For this is how—from Annie's point of view—it feels:
swirl, flux, turmoil. Radical instability. External and internal reference
points vanishing. Unreliably, so that she says of her mother:

"A person I did not recognize answered in a voice I did not recognize."

What matters is Jamaica Kincaid's unsparing honesty. No eider-
down of nostalgia blankets her characters' emotions. No soft focus
blurs Annie's and her mother's escalating savagery toward one another. No saccharine additive blunts the acrid taste of their sarcasm or
helps us swallow their revenge. We are made to feel the all but intolerable fusion of hatred with love. We are thrown back to the time when,
clinging in fear of losing her cherished mother, a girl simultaneously
longs to smite her with murderous blows and behold her lying lifeless
on the ground. On the mother's side, we mark a corresponding greed,
a desperate holding on, an unwillingness to let go—a thicket of impos-
sibilities that translate into kicking the girl brutally away, tyrannizing
her, while seductively luring her back, a painful jumble of contradic-
tory behaviors, none of them fully conscious. Thus *Annie John* plays out
the struggles that take place in a girl's mind not only with respect to
her own internal and external changes but also in response to the
mixed messages coming at her from her mother. It traces her displacement of these messages onto a series of escalating peer relationships,
their conversion into metaphors, and then their resulting collapse into
frantic oscillations of will:

"I missed my mother more than I had ever imagined possible and
wanted *only* to live somewhere quiet and beautiful with her alone, but
also at that moment I wanted *only* to see her lying dead, all withered
and in a coffin at my feet" (my italics). Reading this fateful iteration of

the word *only*, we can grasp the hopelessness of the child's bipartite desire, so desolate and quintessentially human.

Growing up on Antigua as the only child in a family that consists solely of herself, her mother, and her father, a carpenter three and a half decades older than his wife, Annie's entire being as a small girl revolves around her serenely beautiful, competent young mother who in turn lavishes meticulous care and attention on her. Each important object in Annie's life has been fashioned by her parents. She feels they have made her with their own hands.

Her mother treasures garments she has worn long after they are outgrown, garments she has made, and she keeps them, along with other mementos of her daughter's life, in a special trunk. Taking them out periodically, she holds them up, repeats stories about them, and thus reviews the girl's life history with her. Mother and daughter bathe sensuously in scented herbal waters and swim together in the sea, both of them naked, her mother singing to her as Annie clings tightly to her neck, and the screeching wind and birds envelop them as if they were cloistered in some vasty chamber of echoes. We imagine them together as Annie trails her mother on daily shopping rounds, one the worshipful miniature of the venerated other:

"How important I felt to be with my mother . . . When my eyes rested on my mother, I found her beautiful. How terrible it must be for all the people who had no one to love them so and no one whom they loved so, I thought."

Yet, little by little, this paradise withers. One might even say it dies. And thus, *Annie John*, a so-called coming-of-age novel, begins with death. It begins with the death of an imaginary perfect harmony between parent and child, a flawless peace in Eden's garden. And it ends, quite strangely, with a scene that represents a kind of birth, for, having attained her late adolescence at the conclusion of the book, Annie forsakes her island home. We glimpse her sailing to sea, far away from the little dot that is now her mother and about to be swallowed up, obliterated by the inexorable limitations of human vision.

Dying to her childhood, Annie is, in these closing moments of the novel, reborn into young womanhood. But the course has tacked and drifted, and, from first to last, it has taken place in an oneric realm, a time zone of disconnected mental states that zigzag back and forth from dying and burial to parturition and the spilling out of amniotic fluids. Thus, the novel's final sentence reads in part, "as if a vessel filled with liquid had been placed on its side and now was slowly emptying out."

Like so much else in the novel and in childhood and in the experience not only of artists and poets but of each of us and our children, birth and death serve as allegorical markers. Soon little Annie, who thought nobody she herself knew could ever die, must do so herself. Not literally, but in the sense that her child self yields to a succession of newer personae, each with the same name and same rapidly maturing body yet each knowing more, feeling otherwise, and succumbing unevenly and unpredictably to an involuntary process of evolution such that, by the end of the story, this first young Annie we have met has morphed into a sexually developed, ambivalent yet newly independent and confident young woman.

Death, beyond its use as a metaphor for the end of childhood, proves, literally, as we observed in *Ponette*, a subject of endless fascination for children. When she is a small girl, Annie cannot seem to get enough of it. She goes to strangers' funerals alone after school, and the first lie she tells her mother has to do with avoiding detection after attending one of these funerals without permission. She tells her mother that she has failed to pick up the fish for their family's dinner because the fisherman never went to sea that day—a deception that fails when the fisherman, tired of waiting for her, brings the fish to her mother himself. Death and its rituals exert an irresistible attraction. And children, unable to accept finality, are wiser, perhaps, than we. For—as *Ponette* teaches with its imaginary ending—death cannot be final as long as we have memory and history. Still, its very contemplation frightens children. Annie, hearing about a girl whose mother has died, says that it seemed "shameful" for that mother to leave her daughter alone in the world, and we recall similar thoughts expressed by other children. Later on when Annie makes friends with a classmate called Gwen, she conceals from this new friend her deteriorating relations with her mother lest it lower the girl's estimation of her. Any kind of misfortune is better than being forsaken by one's mother, and, of course, as we shall see when we consider *A Raisin in the Sun,* it is not only children who are dependent on their parents: a powerful reverse dependency comes into play as well.

How, then, to account for this obsession with death in childhood? Should it be seen as a counterphobic reaction—a means, in other words, of fending off impending losses by becoming preoccupied with the direst of them? After all, magically, if you can acknowledge the worst, you might protect yourself from the merely bad. "Figures in the Distance," the title Kincaid gives to her novel's opening section, refers to sticklike mourners in a cemetery. When little Annie notices them, she puzzles as to who or what they could be and asks her mother about them. But these "figures in the distance" serve also, I believe, as memory traces remote in time—skeletal phantoms and forerunners of serial relationships that come and go during the narrative, especially the succession of relationships that, for Annie, will dissolve. How apt an image it is. For children, in the earliest stages of drawing, create stick figures when they want to represent the human body graphically on paper (Golomb 2004).

Along with these stick figures on the horizon, Annie, in the same breath, reports to us a host of other impressions from this same ten-year-old summer in the country: the birth of piglets, the feeding of farm animals, the hard-boiled duck eggs she loved to eat, her talking with no one besides her parents, her fear of the dead and her mother's knowledge of people who have died, an idea she reiterates for emphasis to show how impressive this knowledge is to her. Death, birth, eggs, eating, feeding, speaking, and what her mother knows converge in the little girl's mind. Right at the start. Notions only superficially unrelated. For children fuse and blend their impressions in just this way and then make causal connections out of their contiguity, so that, for example, when Annie hears that a certain Doctor Bailey has pronounced a child dead, she feels glad he is not *her* doctor. She further connects the eating of mud with the child's death and links a neighbor's decease and another child's death with eating. Swallowing the wrong substance or too much of it or at the wrong time can make you *dead.* And, similarly, for children, eating connects with pregnancy and birth. What grows visibly and appreciably on women who are soon to give birth are, after all, their bellies, and what makes their bellies grow must surely be food. Through tacit intuitive percepts such as these, Kincaid hints frequently throughout her pages at the deep connections that underlie children's seemingly unrelated notions.

Annie next talks about hands, a central image in the novel and one that carries great symbolic meaning for her since, she believes, she was created by those of her parents. The passages we read invite us to reflect on hands and how we do notice them and how very important they are. *These* hands are her mother's, and they are the ones that bathe her each day, caress and heal her, prepare her food, construct and mend things for her. But after her mother has held a feverish child in them, a child who unexpectedly dies while being held, and after her mother has then taken on the task of preparing this dead child for burial, the familiar hands turn alien. Annie writes that, after this moment, they begin to look different to her:

"I could not bear to have [my mother] caress me or touch my food or help me with my bath. I especially couldn't bear the sight of her hands lying still in her lap."

This viscerally negative reaction, with its eerie atavistic logic, makes perfect psychological sense. A mother's hands, after all, give you everything. They are a pair of hands that, in a special way, belong exclusively to you. Their purpose is to love you. Never must these hands betray you. Never must they turn strange or be contaminated. Never must they touch the body of someone dead, especially not of someone who, before she died, was a little girl like you.

In a protopsychoanalytic treatment of hysteria by Freud's colleague Josef Breuer (Breuer and Freud 1895), we learn of a patient (Anna O.) who, despite extreme thirst, found herself unable to drink from a glass. In a manner analogous to the way Annie's mother's hands turn suddenly repugnant, this girl could not, inexplicably, allow a glass of water to touch her lips. Eventually, under hypnosis, Anna revealed that an English governess had once let a pet lap dog take water from a drinking glass, and the sight had revolted her but she had dared not protest.

Likewise, Annie John withholds her revulsion from her mother. Filled with disgust, she recalls the nauseating smell of bay rum that permeated her mother's hands when she returned each time from the dead girl's house. Through this analogy, we can see the power of unexpressed revulsion when it violates the boundaries of a child's psychic integrity. Different as these situations are, both involve the perception of violation. What matters is that child and adult boundaries don't always match and adults may prove insensitive to a child's discomfort.

Interestingly, when I teach this material to undergraduates, they often ask *why* Anna O. was so upset about a small dog taking water from a glass. To Anna, however, the glass must surely have seemed an object designed exclusively for human use. That is to say, for *her* species alone. The governess had breached the young girl's sense of boundary and self, thus making her uneasy. Similarly for Annie John: her mother's beautiful hands were meant for her alone and for the living, not for the dead. In Anna O.'s case, the English governess was already disliked, and thus what she did added a new layer of repugnance to a previously existing distaste. For Annie John, by contrast, her mother's touch of the dead girl constituted an unfathomable betrayal of love. In both cases a girl's strong feelings are trampled, and the adults involved have no awareness of the child's extreme distress.

Let's imagine for a moment that Anna O. *had* been able to speak to her governess. Suppose she had protested:

"Please, Miss —, don't feed your dog from a glass because it makes me ill," and Annie John had been able to say:

"Mother, I hate it when you touch that dead girl; it scares me."

Would the stories have developed differently? Or, if the girls *had* protested verbally at the time, would their ability to protest have constituted a sign that they were in fact less anxious than we believe they were? Might words of protest at such times *not* allay distress but exacerbate it? In the latter case, might a child's silence (in each case for different reasons) be deemed not merely a result of fear and reticence but also of forbearance born of self-protection and even of cautious and adaptive wisdom? Might the respective silences stem from a tacit intuition that negative feelings on the part of young people are not taken seriously by adults and that any response elicited by protest might prove more unsettling than saying nothing at all? What I mean to convey by these rhetorical questions is that words alone, especially one-sided declarations or protests, cannot carry the day. Trust and mutuality are required. Eyes (and ears) wide open for the feelings of the other.

As we think about these passages in *Annie John* and about the enormous importance to every child of his or her mother's hands, I want to refer to a poem brought to my attention by Anke Lohmeyer of Kassel and Professor Jan Hollm of Ludwigsburg, Germany. "Mother's Hands" (*Mutterns Haende*) is by the German Jewish writer Kurt Tucholsky (1890–1935), who lived in Moabit, the workers' district of Berlin. Composing not in the formal High German, or *Hochdeutsch,* as is usual with poetry in that language, Tucholsky uses a local dialect with phonetic spelling so that, in the original, he achieves a touching, childlike effect.

The poetic speaker addresses his mother.

"You cut slices of bread for us," he reminds her gratefully, and he goes on to recite all that she has done for him and the other children in the family with her hands. She has mopped the floor, sewn for them, slipped candies (bonbons) into their fists, peeled potatoes, sometimes given them a slap (*Katzenkopp*). He reminds her that she has raised eight children but only six of them are still alive. Each stanza ends with the refrain:

"*Alles mit deine Haende*" (Everything with your hands).

The last stanza recalls that her hands were hot and cold but that, now, they are old. Soon you will be in the earth, Tucholsky writes, and we stand here with you now; we stroke your hands (*und denn komm wir bei dir / und streichen deine Haende*).

A mother's hands matter to her children because it is through them that the world is made and unmade. Several months ago, at the Louvre in Paris, I gazed at Leonardo's *Mona Lisa* and focused my attention on her hands. I tried to imagine the painting without them. How much colder it would be and less serene. How patient and relaxed these lovely hands appear, softening the impact of the portrait and tempering its cryptic gaze. Like Tucholsky, Kincaid uses hands—both mother's and father's—as a metaphor for care and love in her novel.

Hands, furthermore, as Kincaid also uses them, have been associated since ancient times with memory. The psalmist, speaking of exile, sits by the rivers of Babylon and weeps when remembering Zion:

"If I forget you, O Jerusalem, let my right hand wither."

Yad Vashem comes to my mind as well, the memorial in Jerusalem for those who died in the Shoah, where *yad,* the Hebrew word for *hand,* is linked with notions of memory and monument.

Such meanings are implicit in the way Kincaid uses the symbol of the hand. Identity is under construction here. Annie's carpenter father makes furniture for their daily lives; her mother's handiwork is ubiquitous. Thus, a rich confluence of signification merges in the moment when Annie recoils from the sight of her mother's hands.

The metaphor recurs. It resurfaces in a hypnotizing key passage in the novel's second section, "The Circling Hand." Older now, and on the threshold of puberty, Annie has started a new girls' school with uniforms and a different cast of characters. In response to her developing pubescent body, her mother has begun to criticize her harshly, as Annie experiences it, and to push her away. This is the section in which Kincaid chants "new . . . new . . . new."

One memorable afternoon, Annie returns home from Sunday school, where she has been awarded top prize as the best student in her Bible class. Buoyed with hope that her prize will stem the tide of estrangement and reinstate harmonious relations between her mother and herself, she enters the house. Hearing sounds coming from her parents' bedroom, she goes to their door. She discovers them lying on the bed together. Her focus goes to her mother's hand, which is making circular movements on her father's back. Just as in the past, when it had touched the dead girl, the familiar hand turns alien. It seems not to be her mother's hand at all. Annie feels that if she could forget everything else, she would never forget her mother's hand as it looks in that moment.

Hypnotized, she stands at the threshold.

Much has been said about the so-called *primal scene,* described by psychoanalysis. At stake for Annie in this riveting moment, however, is something besides accidental exposure to an intimate moment between her parents. Her anguish comes from the fact that, at a time of hope, when she is craving affirmation and a chance to recoup her mother's affection, she gets only her irrelevance. What "the circling hand" means to her is that she is beside the point, she and her vaunted Sunday school prize. She experiences demotion in this moment, demotion by her supremely valued parents just after she has been judged best by others, who do not count. Even beyond demotion: demolition. For Annie sees that, vis-à-vis her mother, at this moment, she has no existence at all. What the hand is *doing* counts less than that it has been withdrawn. It has been given to someone else. Someone more important. Her agony is loss. No longer can she retain the childhood fantasy that she is loved best of all. Beyond rejection, she has been betrayed.

Apportioning love in a family. As if it were a commodity: three potatoes for you, two for you, just one, today, for you. But actually, and probably not solely in postindustrial Western societies, children really *do* want to be loved—as little Max puts it in Maurice Sendak's *Where the Wild Things Are*—"best of all."

Even if we turn back through the centuries to ancient Greece and the tragedies of Aeschylus, we recall how, in that heartbreaking second play of the *Oresteia*, when Orestes makes bold to murder his mother, he does so not only to avenge the death of Agamemnon but also and profoundly because, when he confronts her, Clytemnestra has no answer as to why she sent him away and abandoned him when he was a child. *He needed to be loved by her.* Reading the play with care, we realize that Orestes keeps hoping, right up to the very moment he strikes her, that she will offer him a glimmer of affirmation.

Likewise Oedipus. Revisiting the pages of Sophocles, we see how, at the moment of greatest tension before the revelation of monstrous parricide and incest, this shaken ruler, who is also a son, queries the herdsman who was summoned to tell what happened long ago. What Oedipus wants to know is *who* pierced and shackled his feet when he was a baby and *who* sent him away to die on cold Mount Cithaeron. Stricken with horror, he repeats the herdsman's answer:

"*She* gave it to you?"

Only when he has heard that it was his mother, Jocasta, who gave him away to die does he withdraw to perform the mutilation that will make it impossible for him to see anything ever again.

I am not persuaded, therefore, that feelings like Annie's can be confined to a thin veneer of bourgeois historicity. Annie wants her mother's hands for herself. This cannot be so. Yet, if childhood wishes were acknowledged and valorized, there might be ways to move beyond longing, paralysis, and envy. Picture in your mind's eye Vincent Van Gogh's blackened masterpiece from Nuenen, *The Potato Eaters* of 1885. Here family members share a meal in the direst of poverty. Surely, there must be ways to temper wishes for exclusivity, ways to offer love so that—as it is given and received—it sustains instead of destroys. While writing on the motherless Brontë children in their secluded parsonage in Haworth, West Yorkshire (children who—in the absence of both parents—sketched endlessly and read and wrote and made believe), Elizabeth Gaskell likens their imaginations to potatoes proliferating in a cellar. Could love not prove the same?

As we see from the recurrence of imagery, time assumes an ambient quality in the novel. Mental states disconnect themselves from clock time. Strong reactions recur. A powerful example concerns the onset of Annie's menstrual periods, which she mentions twice in different contexts with nineteen pages in between. In fact, this double mention mirrors the way we often recall an event that overwhelms us. We resist, push back, and then re-remember it but disjointedly. The process is captured by Freud's notion of *Nachtraglichkeit,* whereby an event occurring at one point in time takes on retrospective significance in the light of subsequent events so that, as the new meanings accrue—meanings that were previously latent—we revise our understanding and, in so doing, lose our grip on temporal sequence.

"On the morning of the first day I started to menstruate," we read on page fifty-one. We hear of pains that run up and down Annie's legs and of her mother's less than sympathetic response. We read again on page seventy, "I started to menstruate." This time the event takes place after Annie has prevaricated about the possession of some forbidden marbles. She recounts a dream in which she and a friend inhabit an otherwise deserted island. They eat wild pigs and sea grapes and send signals to passing ships that make them crash. While the girls laugh hysterically, safe on their island, the passengers are all drowned at sea. What do we make of this—both of the repetition and of the difference between the two accounts? Can we connect them?

When Annie feels physical pain, her mother not only deprecates it but jokingly talks about her own first time when she was exactly the same age. Annie squirms under the suspicion that, by virtue of this history telling, her mother wants to bring them together and enforce a kind of twinship. Silently, Annie calls her mother a "serpent." She does this in part because of the momentous physical change itself, which is frightening as well as painful. Her intactness is being assailed. She is bleeding, and her mother, who ought to be protecting her from physical harm, is making jokes. Moreover, Annie needs confirmation of the uniqueness of her own body and her life, right now. She needs to claim the experience, not have it appropriated by her mother. Thus she grows angry, both at her mother's lack of sympathy and at the mother's felt intrusion into what should be her daughter's center-stage role. Annie voices no words of protest, however. She pretends (and actually uses this word) to accept her mother's perceived attempt to unite them.

Many pages later, in the second mention of the event, her previously controlled negative feelings burst forth. Her mother has accused her of hiding some marbles and demands to know where they are. Annie denies possessing them. In an effort to surmount her resistance, her mother embraces the same technique as previously. Unaware that Annie perceives her autobiographical references as infuriating and manipulative, she brings up yet another story from her past. She tells how, as a little girl, she was told to carry a bunch of green figs home from the market on her head and how, as she walked the long road back, the load grew heavier and more painful. She persevered until she reached home and removed the figs from her head. When she did so, a huge black snake crawled out, and she fainted dead away. Moved by this story to a powerful flash of sympathy for her mother and on the verge of revealing the hiding place of the marbles, Annie pulls back. Sensing the story's trap and its snakelike motivation to elicit her confession, she replies chillingly that she has no marbles and has never played with marbles.

Thus, she lies brazenly in her "newly acquired treacherous voice." Immediately, she repeats that she has just begun to menstruate and goes on to tell the sadistic dream about herself and her friend the Red Girl on their island. Why in this dream do the girls take pleasure in doing harm to others? Why do they send confusing signals to ships and then laugh to see them crash on the rocks? What has this to do with what came before? Perhaps we can understand the imagery by noting that Annie herself has been receiving confusing signals from her mother, who both pushes her away and hurts her by refusing sympathy and then beckons her back by setting them up as twins:

"My mother and I each soon grew two faces," writes Kincaid in Annie's voice.

Her dream co-opts and replays that disquieting way of giving mixed signals. Victim is recast as perpetrator. And the turning of tables seems right for this paradigmatic moment when a young girl blossoms passively into a woman. Suddenly, where there had been one woman and one child in the household, there are now two women.

The imagined cruelty in the dream thus releases a measure of the fury that could not be voiced directly by Annie toward her mother. The Red Girl, her friend, participates, I'll venture, because this particular friendship—as we shall see—allows Annie to enact aspects of her inner world that would appall her mother if she knew of them. Sharing responsibility, moreover, for transgressive acts seems magically to reduce one's culpability. Annie's primary dyad with her mother is foundering. In the breach she and the Red Girl have formed a new couple. Her mother's place is ceded to an intimate friend. The girls—in the dream—find their own food on the island; they have no need for mothering. Annie's shrill laughter rings out with manic triumph, and the dream itself seems like a child's game gone mad. Pain, fear, separation from the rest of the world, shame, guilt, and ambivalence swim in eddies within it so that, while the girls collapse in mirth, the passengers of the boats (her mother and Annie both, perhaps, who have always seemed like the entire world) are punished and must die. We have by now been told, apropos, that Annie's parents came to Antigua by boat and, although as first-time readers we do not know it yet, Annie will leave the island by boat at the end of the story. Thus, the dream, altogether *hers,* creates a mise-en-scène that, worthy of a painting, video, theatre piece, or dance, allows her to master, metaphorically, what is happening passively to her body. By means of it, she avenges the world safely for its unwelcome assault.

To return momentarily to the motif of recounting history, Kincaid foregrounds this theme by the symbol of the green and yellow handpainted wooden trunk in which all Annie's childhood treasures are kept. Such histories and artifacts take on altered meanings as children mature. When, at first, Annie is shown the precious relics from the trunk (dresses, booties, certificates), and hears the anecdotes that go with them, she welcomes the experience. She is hungry for the wherewithal to forge her burgeoning identity. We behold her crouching behind her mother, engrossed, as each object from the memory trunk is taken out and its story told. Listening intently, she sniffs her mother's neck and recalls her delight as it gives off delicious scents of lemon, rose, or sage. Kincaid paints for us an idyllic portrait of parent and child, idealized and entwined.

But later on, with the sea change of puberty and the dramatic onset of menstruation, Annie turns away from this joint life. During cataclysmic waves of bodily and emotional upheaval, the same parental stories become chains and weights when wings are wanted. The precious wooden trunk, brought by Annie's mother to the island of Antigua by boat from Dominica when she herself was a girl, alters in meaning for Annie. The trunk is no longer *hers.* It becomes *hers and her mother's.* Finally, it becomes simply *her mother's.* When, toward the end of the novel, Annie's father asks her what she would like him to make for her with his carpenter's tools, she answers unhesitatingly and not without malice, "A trunk." Surprised by this answer, he reminds her that she already has her mother's trunk. Annie repeats her demand for a trunk of her own. Suddenly, a phantasm arises. It is her mother's shadow, looming ominously on a nearby wall to body forth the magnitude of her betrayal. In another stunning specimen of verbal visuality, Kincaid writes:

"I could not be sure whether for the rest of my life I would be able to tell when it was really my mother and when it was really her shadow standing between me and the rest of the world."

History as an enabler and an inspirer, history as a contributor to identity formation, history as a forger of deep familial connections, or history as a prison and a cage? What Kincaid shows us is how the same symbol can morph dramatically in meaning for the growing child while, for the adult parent, it remains static.

Seeking to extricate herself from the dyad with her "serpentlike" mother, Annie feels both ready and unready to snap the bond. Bruised by what she perceives as progressive withdrawals of affection, she winces when her mother refuses to make matching dresses for them anymore. She longs for clamps to screw on in order to make herself stop growing.

Then she secedes. She falls in love with someone else, someone who is *not* her mother. Precipitously, she shifts her affection to a classmate named Gweneth Joseph. Drawing close to this girl, she grows increasingly secretive and duplicitous in her relations with her once adored mother. The kind of secrecy she adopts, moreover, seems different from the reactive secrecy we shall encounter in the next chapter, where Molly, who is growing up in South Africa, also hides feelings and acts from her mother, not—as here—to enforce separation but rather for the opposite reason, to persuade her preoccupied mother to pay attention to her and mimic *her* inscrutable secrecy. Yet, even as I write these words, I can see, in a more nuanced way, that Annie, too, like Molly, keeps secrets both reactively and vengefully, for, as she experiences it, her mother has also rejected her.

While performing brilliantly at school, Annie misbehaves. This way she willfully taints her mother's pleasure in her academic success. What strikes me throughout her long attempt at separation is the relentlessness of her unhappiness. She writes of it as something that was "deep inside me, and when I closed my eyes I could even see it. It sat somewhere—maybe in my belly, maybe in my heart; I could not exactly tell—and it took the shape of a small black ball, all wrapped up in cobwebs." Having been taught from birth that everything she is derives from her mother's devotion (her mother's hands), she needs to wrench herself away. But ambivalence mangles her efforts. Named prefect at school, she plays out her split identity. Sometimes she defends a girl who seems weak, and at other times she is unkind. Seesawing, tacking back and forth, she cannot stabilize. She finds no peace.

Along with Gwen and several other girls from school, Annie goes to an abandoned cemetery to sit among the tombstones. We picture them in shadows, like figures in the distance, furtively whispering secrets to one another about their changing bodies such as how their breasts might appear and grow larger if they rub up against a boy. Murmuring in this ghostly spot redolent of mystery, forbidden by their teachers, and fascinating to Annie ever since the days of her early childhood, they play out their intuitive association of puberty with death. These are, after all, the great involuntary rites of passage. Just as death comes unbidden and uninvited upon us, so does physical maturation, and neither can be kept at bay. Once again, death is juxtaposed with the passing of childhood.

Little by little, as guardedness and suspicion supplant the trust once vested at home, Annie finds that her mother's beauty withers. She sees her mother as small and funny looking and repeats that she will never let her hands touch her again. By contrast, when she describes her best friend Gwen, she repeats the approving phrases once used for her mother, whose lovely mouth had seemed to move up and down as she talked; now her friend's mouth does the same. Gwen's lips and bony, ash-colored knees become objects of veneration. Visuality is of the essence here, and Kincaid captures the way children make these keen observations and transferences and how they actually come to *see* their parents differently. Annie pictures her mother as a crocodile.

What can we say about such a precipitous fall from grace—from idol to demon—and not only on the parent's part from the eyes of a developing child but, importantly, on the child's part with regard to herself, and, of course, on the child's part from the point of view of the parent? Is there a way to temper or forestall it? Must we bear it as a normal element in the process of growing up, chastening but key? Most children allow themselves at least a partial disillusionment with their parents in early adolescence but then, as they come face-to-face with adult life, turn graciously back and bestow a measure of retroactive redemption. *Annie John,* because it reverses course so dramatically, compels us to confront this question head-on. The novel resembles a fairy tale in which a good fairy godmother morphs into a wicked witch. Which, of course, is not the way fairy tales actually work. To protect the sanctity of motherhood, they work, on the contrary, by killing off their birth mothers before the story begins; thus, the idealization of motherly goodness remains intact. Evil stepmothers, on the other hand, run rampant. A real human mother—with her two hands, capable of caressing and smiting—rarely materializes in them (see Bettelheim 1976; and Tatar 1987).

Dependency and idealization are at stake here. Mothers and children both suffer from delusions, and capturing this (at least by half), Yeats pens his wonderful line, "Both nuns and mothers worship images" (from his 1928 poem "Among School Children").

A large part of what makes *Annie John* psychologically brilliant is its relentless demonstration—through the iteration of its vibrant imagery—that both physical and psychic aspects of mother-child reliance are interdependent. This is to say, long after a child needs her mother, a child continues to need her mother. And, perhaps, vice versa.

The transfer, however, of affection in puberty and adolescence from inside to outside the family circle has been well documented in the literature of child psychology, even as far back as the "Dora" case (Freud 1905). Never, I would claim, has it been as vividly described as here, where Kincaid not only shows us the grounds for choice of person for this transfer of affection but also implies that—with all its passion—such friendships rarely last.

Compliant Gwen exists merely to facilitate Annie's first steps out. She brings no novelty, and she represents no risk. She meets with Annie's mother's approval. She is a cipher, the second term in a liaison that works for Annie in the moment but is doomed as a long-term solution or full-fledged exit route. She has been chosen with Annie's flaming ambivalence intact ("My whole mouth filled up with a bitter taste, for I could not understand how [my mother] could be so beautiful even though I no longer loved her"). Beyond the girls' physical intimacy—beyond kissing, touching, pointedly not touching, exclusively possessing one another, and professing fierce loyalty—beyond, in other words, the recapping with each other of the adoring affection they have nearly outgrown with their respective mothers, there is nothing to sustain their dyad.

Even, therefore, as we taste the thrill of this first adolescent friendship, we are aware that a day will come when Annie will write of "my former friend Gwen. We had long ago drifted apart, and when I saw her now my heart nearly split in two with embarrassment at the feelings I used to have for her." Apropos, parents worry over erotically tinged preadolescent friendships, but Kincaid teaches us, in her incandescent hues, that, while they briefly flood consciousness, they are short-lived and reflect symbolically what has occurred in each child's life to date.

Annie, feeling ever more on the outs with her mother, grows bored with Gwen. Moving to another level of alienation, she takes up, in stealth, with a wild tree-climbing, marble-playing child whom she calls the Red Girl. She knows her hygienically minded mother would find this child repugnant, and this, of course, pleases Annie. Kept immaculate by her mother, who continues to wash her hair and insist on two baths daily, Annie notes with glee the unkempt matted hair and filthy fingernails of this girl, her pungent body odor, and especially the fact that, once, when they passed her in the street, Annie's mother voiced contempt.

No need to emphasize the association of red with blood and pain, but we might note a recurrence, for earlier in the novel, when Annie had been so frightened about the mud-eating girl who died in her mother's arms, that dead child was a redhead. Moreover, as Annie goes on in her secret trysts with the Red Girl, the two play sadomasochistic games. Submitting to hard pinches, Annie cries out with pain and then allows her wounded skin to be kissed. In doing so, she recapitulates an earlier childhood liaison with a little neighbor girl, Sonia, whose black body hair she used to pull and tug until that child cried out, whereupon, Annie placated her with sweets paid for with money stolen from her mother's purse. In this furtive new iteration with the Red Girl, that original sadism is reversed; it is she, Annie, who submits to the pinches and is subsequently kissed by her friend. Stealing once again from her mother's purse, Annie, as before, buys ribbons and trinkets for this strange friend, and, unlike the association with Gwen, she meets the Red Girl only in seclusion so that their intimacy is concealed from her mother's watchful eye.

What are we to make of this liaison? How shall we interpret these amorous trysts in an abandoned lighthouse from which the girls look out over the sea (as in Annie's dream)? How to understand not only Annie's erotic play but also her comment that "the sensation was delicious—the combination of pinches and kisses. And so wonderful we found it that, almost every time we met, pinching by her, followed by tears from me, followed by kisses from her were the order of the day"? My reading is that this voluptuous alternation of agony and ecstasy can be seen as a dramatization—with a partner unacceptable to her mother—of the extreme love and hatred Annie is experiencing. Provoked, controlled, and stymied in her relationship with her mother, she creates an alternate arena where passionate feelings can be vented. Moreover, pinching and pulling are done with the *hands*. As is stealing. As is the bestowal of gifts. We already know the supervening importance of hands to this child. Through a dramatic liaison with the Red Girl, Annie stages, recapitulates, and partially *escapes* the oppressively close bond with her mother.

The perverse friendship, with its delirious intensity, forms for Annie a next step in growing up, and, like the romance with Gwen, it cannot last. It exists on a plane of fantasy that provides its significance, and, when that fails, Annie must withdraw, as do so many girls at a certain point, into her own psyche. Thus, what we witness is the way a particular young person tries out, in terms of progressive friendships, some new identities and new ways of being that also reflect her past and catapult her out of the maternal orbit but not definitively. I am not suggesting that the friendships themselves have no importance in their own right. In addition to the psychic resonances they have with regard to Annie and her mother, they are true-life experiences against which Annie measures herself. For example, she speaks at one point of the Red Girl's life as heavenly because *her* mother makes no demands.

Briefly, I want to address the motif of stealing, which begins very early in the book and continues throughout. Stealing, for Annie, as I read her, means breaking rules associated with and maintained by her mother and thus proving to herself again and again that her mother is not omnipotent. It is, after all, her mother from whom she steals, principally, and she exults in the fact that her petty thieveries remain undetected. Her pilfering means something very different, therefore, from Ludo's stealing in the film *Ma vie en rose*. Ludo takes things not to test limits or to challenge authority or to enjoy sweet triumph over an adult or to separate himself from an oppressive bond. He actually wants to *have* what he cannot ask permission for. In Annie's case, what matters is not what she *gets* but the act itself of taking.

I believe, furthermore, that Annie is stealing for a deeper yet not unrelated reason, one that goes beyond simple rebellion. The love she receives from her mother is not unconditional. It is measured. It must be deserved. It can, therefore, never be enough. In this furtive way, by pilfering, Annie takes what is not being given freely to her, but also, in so doing, she betrays repeatedly and poignantly her profound longing to be loved in spite of her "badness," in spite of her dirtiness, in spite of her sexual feelings, her transgressive wishes, her envy, hostility, and doubt. Kincaid, with rich imagery, shows us how what Annie actually steals from her mother gets transformed quickly into little gifts of love that she bestows on others. Thus, as we form and process our mental pictures of these scenes while adding to them from other experiences drawn from life and art, we unravel their metaphoric significance and grasp the purport of this petty thievery. In so doing, we enter more fully into the orbit of the young girl and the recesses of her unquiet heart.

The last chapters of the novel find Annie, after her experiments with friendship, withdrawing into a private world. An existential anguish hovers over her, and she falls ill. Forsaking human companionship, she retreats into a long, solitary illness or adolescent "slumber," a dormant state rather like that of the Sleeping Beauty after she has pricked her finger. During this time, in a fevered trance, she notices a bevy of framed family photographs that have been set up on a table near her sickbed and seem in her delirium to enlarge and diminish alternately in scale and remind her not only of her parents' exclusionary love for one another but of a bitter fight she had with her mother during which she uttered the words "I wish you were dead."

These photographs seem to sweat and emit an odor of impurity, which makes Annie rise from her bed in order to purge them. Washing them with soap and water, she rubs until all the faces have been obliterated and then dusts them with talcum powder so as to rid them of their foulness. The scene is at once surreal, symbolic, and paradigmatic. She ruins the photographs as if, by this mad iconoclastic gesture, she could exorcise their iconicity and eradicate all the memories, shame, and torment they entail. It is as if, with their cleansing and destruction, she could set herself free. Much is condensed in this act—the symbols of water, death, and drowning, her terror of the apotropaic power of images, her wish to clear away guilt and shame, her need to extinguish family history and expunge the many complex feelings that cannot be set right, her need, above all, to demolish the past so as to begin life anew without it.

While ill and existing in this suspended state, Annie receives a visit from her grandmother, Ma Chess, who arrives mysteriously from Dominica to help care for her, and Kincaid gives us another of her unforgettable word-pictures as Annie lies on her side in bed "curled up like a little comma," while her grandmother lies next to her, "curled up like a bigger comma, into which I fit." All the coziness and warmth now gone missing in her relations with her mother come flowing toward her from this loving member of the generation once removed (as we have observed elsewhere in these pages with respect to grandparents). After making her well again, the old woman spirits herself away, reminding us in her wake of all the beneficent visitations from grandparents who arrive from afar, give unstintingly, and who, perhaps because of what we imagine to be their great age, exude foreignness and exoticism—grandparents who, while they are with us, are dearly loved but who, after they leave, are first sorely missed and then quickly forgotten.

Annie knows, upon recovery, that she must get away. On her first day outdoors, she utters the word *never* five times in succession, including the wish "never" to hear her mother's voice again. Longing to be where nobody knows her, far from the island, her childhood, and her parents, she wants "never" to return. On her last day in Antigua, after again rehearsing the word *never*, she reviews all the objects made by her father's hands—the house in which they live, the bed on which she sleeps, her chair, the wooden spoon they use to stir their porridge—and also objects made by her mother's hands—the sheets on her bed, the window curtains, the nightie she wears—and once again she knows for certain that she must leave. Her parents are together; she is apart. A tall young woman now, she walks with the two of them from the house to the pier or "jetty," and, as she walks, she passes through, as she puts it, the years of her life.

At parting, her mother clasps her with tears streaming down her cheeks and crushes her so hard that Annie stiffens suspiciously:

"Still holding me close to her, she said, in a voice that raked across my skin, 'It doesn't matter what you do or where you go, I'll always be your mother and this will always be your home.'"

Yet, as the boat pulls away from shore and heads for the open sea, the last object Annie makes out is a disappearing dot, a figure in the distance that is her mother's form, waving wildly to her, and she waves wildly back. When she goes inside her cabin finally and lies down, there is an almost audible sigh, a profound sorrow and a letting go, a sense of release and a rush of boundlessness, an oceanic sensation, an opening out to universal identification—a birthing into some vast and infinite unknown.

Here the story ends. I close my tattered copy of *Annie John* and reflect on the months I have spent writing about it, not to mention the years I have spent rereading it and teaching it. I see it has flung me back, without mercy, into the forgotten depths of my own girlhood and dared me to brave family photographs labeled with white ink and crowquill pen on deckled black pages in leather-bound albums made by my own mother's hand. It has made me look once more at a little girl with braids and unsmiling eyes. Tagged with my name, I hardly know her. The book pushes me back in time and makes me want to understand her. What is she feeling, wishing, and thinking about while somebody points the camera at her? She hates to have her picture taken. She thinks she isn't pretty. She says nasty things to her mother, and she runs away from home. Does she, like Annie, purposely misbehave partly to test her mother's love, even though, like Annie, she already knows it won't work? Soon there won't be any more chances for this little girl to find out. In a few years, her mother will be dead. What about Annie John? Did she go back to Antigua and hear her mother's voice again? In one important way we know the answer because the book itself is a return. As for the little girl in the album, her answer is positive, too, for her mother's voice has become a part of her own.

The Mother-Artist

Oh, Mama, just look at me one minute as though you really
saw me.
—EMILY, FROM *OUR TOWN* (THORNTON WILDER)

The intense and very much admired New York painter Elizabeth
Murray (1940–2007) was welcomed onstage at a conference on
film, art, dreams, and creative processes where I was also an invited
speaker. Immediately upon arriving at the podium, Murray informed
her audience how uncomfortable and alienated she feels when she is
publicly presented. She has difficulty recognizing herself, she told us,
in the strange pictures that form in her mind while she listens, mentally stitching together the patches of information furnished by
strangers' recitals of her accomplishments.

Sitting in a dim hall listening to her words, I began to remember my
mother—of years ago—and uncanny sensations returned.

Mine was a mother-artist. I do not mean to imply by this that she was
a person who paints, writes poetry, or plays the piano (although actually she did all of the above) but someone rather who spends her days
creating her children. My mother did this in part by focusing her attention on the details of our appearance. Not a speck escaped her
gaze. She carefully dressed my sister and me in pastels, plaids, and
pleats, in neatly ironed dresses and pinafores, with evenly turned-down

Arthur Rackham (1932), *Gerda and the Little Robber Girl,* illustration
from "The Snow Queen" by Hans Christian Andersen. (Courtesy
Mount Holyoke Library.)

socks to go with them and freshly polished shoes. She brushed and braided my long brown hair and tied the plaits with ribbons and taught me to sit with my legs close together, crossed at the ankles, and my back straight and my elbows off the table. I was admonished to move my soup spoon in an "away" rather than a "forward" motion and never to stare. I was meant to be polite to strangers and forbidden to use an entire roster of "naughty" words.

Strangely enough, the little girl my mother saw before her when she studied me critically each morning before I left for school was a different child from the one I really was. I knew and recognized that perfect little stranger who existed in my mother's mind, but to me she seemed a phantom, an enemy, or a guest. I did not even want to be her except once in a while when the stakes were high (as on occasions when there seemed to be the chance of sitting next to a favorite uncle at the dinner table or of receiving an elaborate gift). Inside the envelope of skin scrubbed pink by my mother resided another small person—messy, greedy, selfish, envious, and tyrannical—a lumpish child who felt lonely, miserable, and ashamed all at once and also fiercely stubborn.

Somehow, listening to the artist describe her painful discomfort at being introduced in public helped me to formulate a new idea about why I was often naughty and disobedient, hell-bent on provoking my mother. What Elizabeth Murray taught me by her open avowal before the audience was, I realized suddenly, that I must have been trying desperately to get my mother's attention and make her see through the camouflage of ribbons, lace, and starch. I wanted her to notice me and find me, to see me as I really was in my own head—feisty, insolent, unlovable, but clever, too—and to love me just the same. I wanted her to love me for my imperfections, not in spite of them and not in denial of them. But, of course, my misbehavior produced disastrous results. In the grief-laden moments that inevitably followed disobedience, I *did* get seen, at least momentarily. But not seen with the unconditional love I craved.

By the time I had reached adulthood, my mother-artist had succeeded. She had molded me so thoroughly that I found I actually wanted to be seen in costume. In mask and masquerade. Sophisticated,

up-to-date, adult equivalents of black patent leather Mary Janes, crino-
lines, and saddle shoes had become a necessity. By then, I was convinced that actresses are loved *only* when they are onstage. Eventually,
as a scholar at the Getty Center in Santa Monica, I was informed one
embarrassing day by a formidable doyenne of film studies that aca-
demia is *not* a dinner party; likewise, a stern philosophy professor at Co-
lumbia chastened me for being like a belle who cannot bear lulls in
conversation. Such disconcerting traits are traceable directly to my
mother-artist, for it was she who touted throughout my childhood the
supreme value of gentility.

Somewhere, however, and not always completely well sequestered,
there lurks a moody, muddy, smudge-faced, uncombed figure who resembles Arthur Rackham's illustration for the little Robber Girl from
Hans Christian Andersen's *The Snow Queen*. She hides away, alienated,
like Elizabeth Murray's private self. Occasionally, she peeks out to
make nasty faces at the world, but then quickly, like the wicked child in
the Haggadah, she beats a hasty retreat, withdrawing out of sight.

If a mother-artist's clay survives her death, and if it has been air-
dried only and thus escapes the irreversible fires of the kiln, it will
probably retain some of its original malleability, some of its capacity to
continue altering its shape, at least in theory. Every artist's product,
moreover, even a mother-artist's, moves out of the studio one fine day
and into the wider world, where it lives, in spite of and because of what
it has been given, a life of its own. Children grow up, to an extent.
Some of them even become artists.

Counting on You

We were kept very separate. They said they were trying to protect us, but really it was easier, simpler, not to have to explain things to children . . .
— SHAWN SLOVO

She was willing to pay the price for her own activism. But the children? She tried to put them out of her mind, but of course she could not. Their fate seemed as fragile as her own.
— GLENN FRANKEL

When a film set in South Africa under apartheid was released, one of my daughters asked if I would see it with her. We went together, and it moved us both deeply. Jennifer saw it mainly as a clear-eyed depiction of political turmoil and brutality, a searing portrait of lives distorted by inhumanity and unreasoning racial prejudice. We both felt it dramatized the painful conflicts faced by mothers (and daughters) who attempt to do important public work in a world that continues to stereotype, constrict, and censure them even when they are, at the same time, trying to perform ongoing duties at home, where feminine responsibilities have traditionally been vested.

This was the background of my first exposure to *A World Apart* (1988), a film as timely today as when it was originally released. Its set-

A World Apart (1988), directed by Chris Menges. *Shown from left:* Jodhi
May, Barbara Hershey. (Courtesy of Photofest.)

ting is the South Africa of 1963, Johannesburg, between the
Sharpeville Massacre of 1960, when the African National Congress was
banned, and the Rivonia trials of 1964, when Nelson Mandela and others were sentenced to life imprisonment on Robben Island. The
screenplay is by Shawn Slovo, eldest daughter of the eminent South
African activist-journalist Ruth First, whose life she has fictionalized in
it (as the character Diana Roth), and the prominent Communist anti-
apartheid activist Joe Slovo (fictionalized as Gus Roth). Slovo herself,
depicted as a young girl, is called Molly in the film. Mining her own
memories, Slovo also draws on her mother's memoir, *117 Days: An Account of Confinement and Interrogation under the South African Ninety-Day
Detention Law* (First 1965).

By way of background, Slovo's parents belonged to a circle of immigrant second-generation Jewish intellectuals and activists in Johannesburg who opposed apartheid with vehemence and who, in part be-

cause they saw communism as the only color-blind political option, joined the Communist Party in the 1940s and 1950s. (For additional background, see—in addition to Mandela 1995—Frankel 1999.) The activist group with whom the Slovos were associated included prominent figures such as Mandela, Walter Sisulu, and Rusty (Lionel) Bernstein who became the model for Nadine Gordimer's character Burger in her celebrated novel *Burger's Daughter* (1979).

Although the filmed story ends with a moving scene of reconciliation between mother and daughter, the audience is informed in a text message onscreen that Ruth First was later murdered. After her prolonged detention in prison, her subsequent house arrest, and the banning of her writings, all of which are depicted onscreen, she finally left South Africa. Taking her children with her, she settled in London. Several years later she returned to Africa alone to continue working against apartheid. It was then that the vengeful South African Special Branch police murdered her. In 1982, they planted a time bomb in her mail, causing a fatal explosion. By this time, her daughter, Shawn, future auteur of the film, was in her thirties.

In keeping with the film's title, I want to focus once again, in the pages that follow, on the tearing *apart* of a mother and daughter. What happens here, however, is different from the tearing apart that engaged us in the previous chapter devoted to Jamaica Kincaid's novel *Annie John*. Here the family rupture occurs in a context of societal fragmentation—that is to say, in a context of racial, national, ideological, cultural, and linguistic breakdown. The film bares distortions that occur and pain that results when the normally uneasy process of early adolescent separation of daughter from mother takes place in a sociopolitical milieu that induces, exacerbates, and derails it all at once. Although many years have passed since Slovo's film appeared and won its accolades at the Cannes Film Festival, and although political changes have occurred in the interim both in South Africa and in the world at large, there is far too much, worldwide, that has *not* changed, and that makes this film as relevant today as it was when it first appeared.

A World Apart focuses on the one particularly delicate moment in the rapport between a mother and daughter that occurs when a girl is on the verge of becoming a woman and when, consequently, there must be a renegotiation, more or less peaceful in nature, of power relations within the family. It is worthwhile to point out, in passing, that, while this shift is triggered physically by the girl's first menstruation, it may come earlier or later psychologically, and it is played out dramatically in some form between each mother and daughter.

Several Jewish women of Eastern European background have told me they recall being ritually slapped across the face by their mothers when they began to menstruate. Although I have been unable to discover any religious explanation, if there is one, for this custom, it certainly concerns the theme of power. As the daughter enters into her own womanhood, her mother reasserts authority, the slap indicating that the existing hierarchy in the family will continue unchanged. The slap may also betoken a silent maternal admonition concerning the new dangers of sexual intimacy with boys and men. In Yemen, another Jewish custom involves the mother placing her daughter's hands into a bowl on the day of her first menstrual period. The mother then pours melted butter over the girl's hands and arms, and she breaks chunks of pita into the bowl to indicate that, from now on, blessings will flow from her hands to her daughter's and from her daughter's hands onward, so that charity will pass from both of them to the poor. In sharp contrast to the slap, this ritual seems to imply that a Yemenite mother, rather than reinforcing her power, seeks to share it beneficently with her maturing young daughter. Rather than construing power as the capacity to strike, the second custom construes power as the capacity to give. In contemporary American life, there are no widely accepted rituals to mark this momentous event in a girl's life. Shame, fear, and confusion still attend it in some quarters, and many girls would benefit from some kind of formal acknowledgment. Because women have been oppressed cross-culturally and because ambivalence surrounding female sexuality is widespread, the menarche has not been honored everywhere as a rite of passage. *A World Apart* causes us to consider, by indirect association, that this phenomenon deserves reflection. It stimulates us to encourage creative measures, at least on the part of individual mothers toward their own daughters.

To Molly, the child protagonist of *A World Apart,* maternal power manifests itself in the form of the capacity to withhold information. Molly's mother, as Molly is aware, is keeping secrets. Molly resents this and cannot fathom it. We, of course, know the reason. Because Diana is a prominent public figure, a brazenly outspoken antigovernment journalist whose life is in constant danger, she cannot reveal her whereabouts and other facts to Molly. She conceals information to protect the girl and avoid frightening her. Should the police question her at any time, the girl must know nothing that could prove damaging to her, to the family, or to others. Molly, however, is precisely at the point in her growing up when she needs to feel trusted by her mother. She craves a base from which *she* can be the one to break away on her own terms as her development dictates. Her mother's professional constraints and the exigencies of the society in which they are living do not alter this fundamental need. Thus, she feels infantilized and distrusted. Meanwhile Diana, totally absorbed in her work, fails to grasp her daughter's discomfort.

Secrecy within the family arises in nearly every chapter in this book. Principally, it is foregrounded in Rosler's film, *Mendel,* where we observed its results taking form in a boy's symptomatic behavior and fantasy life as he tries to understand a traumatic past no one can make sense of. Dora, Freud's adolescent patient, mentioned earlier, feels wounded and resentful that information about her parents' intimate lives is withheld from her and falsely redescribed. Anne Frank, in the unexpurgated wartime diaries now made public, records secrets kept by her mother and herself from one another. In Kincaid's *Annie John,* the concealments also operate in both directions—mother from daughter and daughter from mother.

Secrecy proves a perennial theme in the relations between parents and children. Here, once again, we will see how, in retaliation for parents' "secrets," whatever their content is or is thought to be, and however legitimate or illegitimate, and also in order to secure newly forming boundaries from encroachment, preadolescent children close themselves in. They hide. They contrive secrets of their own. They externalize their need for privacy by means of locked journals, bolted doors, whispering voices, coded languages, and even, sometimes, by running away from home.

In *A World Apart,* Molly tries to get back at Diana by clamming up. She refuses at one point to tell her mother about a conversation she has just held with the headmistress at her school. Explicitly, she conceals this information as a retaliatory measure, but we cannot help noticing how political conditions complicate and aggravate her normal development. For Diana, secrets are the price of safety. For Molly's father, safety means vanishing altogether. He has been forced underground. We watch him kiss Molly good-bye at the start of the film, and we never see him again. What compounds his loss to the family and makes it doubly unendurable is that it cannot be discussed. Not only can Diana not tell her children where their father is or reassure them about his return, but she herself is in darkness, just as they are. Thus, the developmental imperatives, already sensitive, are fraught with extra baggage. The ante is upped, and we in the audience are left, just like the characters onscreen, to cope as best we can with our anxiety.

We see how the necessity for silence, brought on by these political considerations, increases a child's sense of isolation. Early adolescence can be a lonely time. For girls, vast bodily changes and a newfound distance from their mothers frequently confer a sense of estrangement. Aliens to themselves, some find that their familiar external surrounds also morph into unrecognizability. Molly feels doubly abandoned by Diana, who seems to care more for complete strangers than for her own daughter. This perception fits with the developmental path as well since, as girls pass through puberty, they often feel they are losing their privileged status with their mothers (a phenomenon we saw illustrated in Jamaica Kincaid's novel). Their former status was conferred on them partly because, as very little girls, they were often compliant with, adoring of, and nonthreatening to their mothers. Preadolescent girls, in fact, sometimes retreat to this position. They try to stem the tide of individuation by retaining elements of girlishness. Others plunge headlong into rebelliousness and welcome their adolescence, where a different kind of privileged status beckons, a status that may involve hetero- or homosexual exploration with peers and prelude a close alliance with their mothers. The latter option, however, is fraught with trouble for Molly. As a child of white, Communist, Jewish agitators in a country controlled by Afrikaner racists, she finds herself an outsider. There is no like-minded peer group to which she can turn, no safe family home in which to grow up and grow out of. Her plight is evinced in an early scene in the movie in which we observe her in a social situation.

Molly's best friend Yvonne belongs to a well-to-do Afrikaner family that upholds the prevailing white supremacist, establishment ideology and is anti-Communist. At a gala party thrown by Yvonne's parents in their imposing mansion, the two girls, decked out in elegant party dresses, their hair specially coiffed for the occasion, participate in the adult social function. Molly's behavior is revelatory. Whereas Yvonne— after being boisterously caressed and admired by her buxom, blonde, overbearing mother—boldly asks the boy standing next to her to dance, Molly does not follow suit. She avoids looking at the boy who stands near her. Awkward in this debonair world, she wistfully watches Yvonne go off to dance and then retreats from the party. She wanders away into the kitchen, where hired black women are cooking and serving, and she diffidently accepts their offer of something to eat. Molly feels more at ease sitting in the kitchen in her party dress nibbling hors d'oeuvres than asking a boy to dance. In this way, she pulls back from adolescence and at the same time imitates her mother's comfort and involvement with the nonwhite population. Her absence from the party does not go unnoticed, however, by Yvonne's mother, who bustles after her and, with her kindly but imperious manner, orders her out of the kitchen and back once more into the party. There Molly is humiliated by an unprovoked verbal attack on the part of Yvonne's boorish father, who seems incapable of controlling his racist, anti-Communist, and possibly anti-Semitic prejudices.

In the Roth family, all direct expression of emotion must be stifled. In part, cultural norms are at play here, but beyond them it is clear that Molly's hurt feelings toward her mother cannot be easily expressed. After passage of the infamous Ninety-Day Act, under which the South African Special Branch police were given license to arrest and detain citizens merely on suspicion of anti-apartheid activity, they burst into the Roth home and haul Diana off to jail.

Molly and her two sisters, at this point, find themselves abandoned and parentless. They are left in the sole care of a severely overworked hired woman Elsie, and their frail maternal grandmother, whom Diana calls at the last minute. There is, now, no more mother to get upset with. By way of a substitute, Molly acts out her feelings against her visiting grandmother. She behaves with such rudeness and is so oppositional that the beleaguered lady, worried deeply about her own imprisoned daughter, Diana, looks at her granddaughter and says:

"Sometimes I think you have no heart."

But Molly is far too troubled to care. She has resorted instinctively to the mechanism of trying to make herself feel better by causing someone *else* to feel as helpless, as left out, and as unloved as she does. She also behaves harshly to her little sisters. Because the only people in the world who count are giving her no attention, namely, her mother and father, she cannot give it to anyone else. Lacking nurturance by them, she has no resources with which to nurture the younger children. Nastily, she shoves them out of her room. In each scene—with her grandmother at the dining table and with her sisters—Molly's unkind behavior constitutes a reenactment of her own emotional plight. With uncharacteristic hostility, she perpetrates on those around her what she is forced to endure passively in the mother-daughter relationship.

As we watch her in these scenes, we can see she is experimenting and trying, albeit maladaptively, to find a way to survive. She is also, in her spitefulness, "identifying with the aggressor" because her mother's inattention seems to her like willful neglect. Appalled at her insensitivity to the other family members both older and younger than she and equally vulnerable, we simultaneously sympathize with her and grasp the roots of her temporary callousness.

Our ability as an audience to recognize the complexity of her situation at this point and thus to withhold any negative judgment of her is a gift conferred by the film. It is a gift conferred by the medium itself and artistic representation in general. Because we have no advocacy role to perform here and no personal self-interest to promote, we are free, if we can, to practice an aesthetic detachment that enables us to grasp more than can a single character within the drama at any given moment. This way of beholding, a way that might be analogized to Immanuel Kant's *free play of the imagination* or to Freud's *evenly hovering attention,* liberates us to reflect even as we watch.

Apropos of the suppression of feeling, the imperative to keep emotions under control is made explicit when the film starts. Under cover of night (to avoid discovery), Molly's father leaves his family, possibly forever. His destination is unknown. In bed in her pajamas, anxiously wakeful, Molly hears the rumble of a car motor. She jumps up and runs outdoors. In a brief, heartbreaking scene, Gus Roth's final directive to his aching young daughter is:

"Be cheerful."

Diana reiterates this jarring message later on when, referring to the police, she instructs her children grimly never to cry in front of *them.* Molly's grandmother also requires the squelching of emotions. Allowed finally to take the children to visit Diana in prison, she turns to her daughter and asks:

"Are you cracking up? We're counting on you."

Interestingly, those precise words were actually uttered by Ruth First's mother, Tilly, in the real-life circumstances on which the film is based (Frankel 1999). Thus, a conspiracy of silence with regard to emotions, as well as information, is imposed and observed. Under conditions of tyranny, such as were in place in South Africa, silence works insidiously to wrench people apart from one another. Even more treacherously, silence forces people to part from themselves. By not acknowledging one's own actual feelings and not testing them in an interpersonal arena, an individual can lose touch with aspects of him- or herself. Having forfeited wholeness and a sense of personal integrity, one becomes increasingly vulnerable to destructive forces from without and from within. Diana learns this lesson painfully in jail, and, at the very end of the film, in her poignant reconciliation with Molly, she demonstrates that she has had a flash of insight into this particularly virulent consequence of oppression.

Throughout the action of the film, mention is rarely made of Gus Roth. Yet his absence, his not being there for both wife and children, pervades the story. He cannot help them. He cannot protect them. In effect, he fails them. And most frightening to characters and audience alike is the unvoiced uncertainty over him. Nobody is permitted to betray a syllable of anxiety, to say he is missed, to wonder aloud whether he is safe or even still alive. And because all such fears and questions are proscribed, there can be no comfort within the family. No solace given and received between mother and children. His figure looms like a spectral shadow over the lives of those left behind. His prominent nonpresence reminds us of absent fathers in other contexts (war, exile, poverty, illness, divorce, and death) who are gone and unmentioned. What is especially important to note here is that from a child's point of view an absent father is just that. Not there. Gone away. The reasons matter little. A threatening societal milieu, whether in South Africa or elsewhere, thus distorts and magnifies a situation that is already difficult and renders it unendurable.

Let's turn and compare two of the three mothers who are depicted in the film; the third mother will be considered a little farther on. At first glance, Molly's and Yvonne's mothers seem an almost perfect contrast. Think in terms of the *good* mother/*bad* mother divisions we find in fairy tales between, say, a beneficent fairy godmother, and all those wicked witches and evil sorceresses. Very early, right at the beginning of the film, we are introduced to Yvonne's mother, who has already been described as a full-figured, blonde, Afrikaner matron. In this scene, she arrives in her large white sedan to pick up her own daughter and Molly after classes at their all girls' private day school. Parenthetically, color is used throughout the film to emphasize the racial divides that have broken the country apart. As this woman and the two schoolgirls traverse crowded Johannesburg streets in their ostentatious automobile, a ghastly accident occurs in which a black man is nonchalantly run over by a vehicle that never stops; the man lies bleeding on the pavement while pedestrians and traffic rush indifferently by.

Horrified, Molly wants to stop the car immediately, to get out and do something about the situation, but Yvonne's mother refuses and drives impassively on, saying, "I don't want to get involved." What do we have here? A mother who is *good*, perhaps, in the sense of being available to fetch her daughter and her daughter's chosen friend from school, but who is *bad* by virtue of her shocking unconcern over what happens, apparently, to anyone else, to anyone outside her charmed circle, a circle demarcated by race and class.

This mother of Yvonne's (who is never named in the film) drops Molly off, now, at her own mother's journalism office a few minutes later, and we see another kind of good/bad parent. Wholly preoccupied with the oppressed people of her country, Diana manifests utter disinterest in her daughter's arrival. She is too busy to greet Molly with the remotest semblance of warmth. She has no time to spare. She will not even let Molly tell her what has just happened in the street. The girl falls silent, and her head droops to one side. What is of particular interest is that—from Molly's point of view—*both mothers have behaved exactly the same way*. Both of them have ignored her and refused to pay attention to what has upset her so terribly. Yvonne's mother refused to stop the car, and her own mother will not let her speak.

Although the women react as they do for completely different reasons, their behavior—from the child's point of view—registers as equivalent and bitterly disappointing. Molly needs to process what has happened before her eyes, and no one will let her do so. Yet, at the same time, we have the demonstration, in these two women—in these very scenes—of a polarization that mirrors one of the many polarizations mythologized in our culture. Women are either at home or they are not. And, even today, they are idolized or demonized accordingly. Their so-called goodness or badness is still racked up accordingly. How far have we come in our fantasies from Dickens's notorious Mrs. Jellyby of *Bleak House*, the quintessential female do-gooder, whose willingness to sacrifice everything for the people of Borrioboola-Gha means that her own children stumble about in abject neglect with dripping noses, torn clothes, and bloody knees?

Sharp contrasts between Diana Roth and Yvonne's unnamed mother are further painted in visual terms. In contrast to the fair, mirthful, affectionate flamboyance of the latter, Diana is dark, slender, moody, and aloof. Interestingly, and very authentically, both mothers manage to aggravate and embarrass their daughters, Diana by not being present at all for Molly and Yvonne's mother by being overly present and intrusive: she practically smothers Yvonne, for example, in the previously mentioned party scene. It is also not without relevance, and not unrelated to the issues of color that pervade the film, that the fictional Roths are Jews like their real-life counterparts. Thus, the blonde hair of Yvonne's mother contrasts vividly with the black hair of Diana Roth and might even, for some viewers, invoke the legendary figures of Marguerite and Shulamite in Paul Célan's haunting 1947 poem "Todesfuge."

The women are in some ways foils for one another, but they are also twinned. We see them as antithetical in their spheres of function. Diana seeks power by working in the larger arena of her splintered society; Yvonne's mother withdraws from public life and confines herself to the home. She tries lamely, by avoidance ("I don't want to get involved"), to shield herself from what is going on in the world outside her circle and maintains, by denial, the fragile bubble she has blown. The two women are twinned, of course, in the complexity of their relations with their respective daughters, and, what is additionally significant, they are both—while strong—stunningly helpless in the face of male aggression.

What can we learn by juxtaposing them? The folly, in part, of thinking in binary terms. For, after all, except from an infant's need-based perspective, there are no exclusively good or bad mothers but simply women who make choices and have choices foisted on them. By offering these extremes, the film invites us to make use of them and take them as touchstones by which to gauge the choices we make in our own lives. We shall register the likenesses, therefore, as well as the more obvious differences between these two mothers.

Male tormentors drive Diana to the brink of suicide. After she is taken to jail under the Ninety-Day Act, she manages to be brave for a long time but finally reaches a point, as prisoner, when the relentless cruelty of the police interrogators persuades her she cannot go on. She writes a suicide note and tries to take her own life.

Yvonne's mother, forceful as she is, cannot protect Molly from the bigotry and irrational rage of her own husband. This is demonstrated in a scene in which, after Diana has been imprisoned, Molly finds herself alone in the house. Forlorn but hopeful, she telephones Yvonne, even though most of the children at their school have by now turned openly against her. There is no answer, but Molly decides to walk over to Yvonne's anyway, a somewhat daring course of action for this very shy girl, especially in a social milieu where it is not considered polite to appear uninvited at another person's gate.

As background for the scene, we need to know that, by this time in the story, Molly is in despair. Her father's disappearance and escape have now become public knowledge, as are her mother's notorious seizure and detention by the police. As a result, the children at her school have come, gradually, to shun her, and she is being cruelly ostracized. Even her former friends call her names. Her once beloved Yvonne among them. Hoping to rekindle this important friendship and mend the rift she cannot fully comprehend, Molly arrives hopefully at the imposing gates to the grounds of the palatial mansion where she has previously been a welcome guest. Rather than being greeted with warmth and asked in, however, she is subjected to a stream of abuse. Yvonne's brutish father appears, and, over the protestations of his wife, he insults Molly, bullies her, and chases her away up the road in a scene of gratuitous sadism.

Thus, neither Diana nor Yvonne's mother, strong women and powerful as they undoubtedly are in their own domains, proves a match for male aggression—either at home or in the public sphere. I want to point out, furthermore, that in the scene just described all the children nearby are implicitly watching and learning, for we may assume that Yvonne and her other friends are witnesses to her father's brutality and its effect on the terrified Molly. None of them is deaf or blind to the behavior of adults. As the line goes from Stephen Sondheim and James Lapine's musical *Into the Woods*, "Children will listen." What parents say and do, and what they fail to say and do, is observed and, on some level, recorded by their own and others' children.

With regard to mothers bad and good and to Diana's mothering in particular, let's go to another scene early in the film before Diana has been arrested and taken to jail. Molly and Yvonne are still close friends at this point, and Yvonne has come to play at Molly's house. The two girls and Molly's younger sisters are all cavorting on the ample grounds of the Roths' homestead. Two strangers, both men of color, arrive unexpectedly on the lawn, one of them being, as it turns out, their housekeeper Elsie's activist brother Solomon, who has just been released from prison. The men ask to see Mrs. Roth, and Molly obediently interrupts her play to lead them to where her mother has been working behind closed doors. When Molly knocks, Diana opens the door, frowns at her, and rudely chastises her for interrupting.

When Diana looks past Molly and sees the two men, her expression abruptly melts from a stiff scowl into a charming smile. Ushering them into her sanctuary, she closes the door roughly behind them without a word for Molly. She seems completely oblivious of her daughter's hurt look and drooping shoulders.

What is the message here? Can it be true that to be a caring person outside the home one must be an insensitive one within it? Is this a model that perdures? I would argue that such a model does perdure and that it even pertains to fathers as well as mothers, although it is used far more prevalently against mothers. Like all crude dichotomies, it proves doubly vicious. Damaging in obvious ways to women (and men) who try to juggle multiple spheres of functioning as best they can, it is a model that hurts children too. Consider how fluctuating and complicated role models and identifications become in early adolescence, when, as Erik H. Erikson (1968) points out, identity itself must be renegotiated. Congruity with parents, however strong or weak, comes, under the sway of puberty, to erode and crumble (as in Kincaid's *Annie John*). Dichotomous models of adult functioning do harm. Rejected and confused by her real mother, where can Molly turn? Unlike Annie John, she is barred from turning to her peers. There is, for her, no group of friends with whom she can work out her differences from, and likenesses to, her mother.

Not surprisingly, Molly turns to the family housekeeper, Elsie. Elsie is thus the third important mother depicted in this film. Wise, kind, and gentle, Elsie, however, as a woman of color, is almost totally disempowered. Separated from her own children, who live in poverty in Soweto, she has accepted a residential service position in the Roths' home strictly in order to support and supply a livelihood for those faraway children. Given the state of apartheid, there is little else she is permitted to do. Evidently, she is the mother most destructively affected by what is going on in the world around them, and it is true that, as an audience, we are not made privy to the extent of her suffering, just as we know very little about the life of Yvonne's family; Shawn Slovo focuses steadily, as screenwriter, on the mother-daughter relationship in which she herself took part.

Molly retreats to Elsie's small room, sits on her bed, and learns a few words of her Bantu language and how to sing some of her songs, and at one point Elsie shows Molly photographs of her absent children and repeats their names. Molly looks at them and at Elsie and asks gently: "Are you sad?" Thus, a bond grows between the two of them, but it is, to some extent, a bond of the helpless.

Turning to Elsie is also Molly's way not only of finding a substitute *good* mother in place of her seemingly *bad* one but also, paradoxically, of identifying with her own mother and of obliquely connecting with her in her absence by getting close to one of the very same people Diana is trying so earnestly to help. On Elsie's side, a certain painfully acquired wisdom tempers whatever she may harbor of understandable anger, caution, and fear. She recognizes that the conditions fragmenting her life are not the fault of the family with whom she is living. She feels no resentment toward Molly but offers her a semblance of the motherliness she is prevented from giving on a daily basis to her own children. At the same time, she, more than Molly, tacitly understands the unwritten boundaries of their closeness and the gulfs that separate them.

As we think about this relationship, we might picture in our mind's eye all the many women of color who continue to push prams in New York's Central Park or in the garden of the Place des Vosges in Paris or in London's Hampstead Heath and elsewhere. How many of those women, like Elsie, are the mothers of faraway children who are missing them and for whom they yearn? How many of those women, con-strained likewise by race, politics, ideology, and poverty, are forced to bestow upon the children of others the love they would so much rather be giving to their own?

When Molly goes with Elsie to visit her family in Soweto, we are made to see how the substitute identification she is trying to forge breaks down. Elsie is not Molly's mother, and the black community cannot make up to her for what is missing in her own life. Just as, in the party scene at Yvonne's house, she was chased out of the kitchen and sent back to the white folks' gathering, likewise, in the scene in Soweto, she fails, despite the warmth of her hosts, to fit in. Ill at ease, she sits po-litely at their simple table at dinnertime, but she cannot bring herself to eat the chicken foot she finds floating in her soup, even when it is explained to her that this is considered a delicacy. She observes the re-spectful attitude Elsie and her family display toward their aged, blind grandfather, a trenchant foil for her own discourteousness toward her visiting grandmother.

Elsie's brother Solomon, who is there with them that night and knows how hard Molly's mother has worked on behalf of his people, wants especially to make Molly feel welcome and accepted. Intending to praise her, he says to her and of her, "Molly is strong like her mother." His words, however, fall flat on her ears. What can Molly make of such praise? All she hears is that, even here, even in Soweto, she can-not escape her destiny. Even within the black community and far from home, she hears words that thrust her back into the place where she needs to be but is finding it so difficult to be.

In terms of warmth and affection, Elsie functions rather more like Yvonne's (partially) *good* mother than like Diana Roth, who is cold, but she, too, is flawed as a refuge for Molly. She has been rendered—be-cause of the color of her skin—far more powerless than the other two women and ultimately, therefore, proves an unsatisfactory role model for the confused young girl.

We explored the significance of close friendships in early adoles-cence to some extent in the preceding chapter. Cultivating an intimate "best friend" often helps a girl to segue gracefully out of her mother's orbit before developing mature social and sexual relations of her own. In Molly's situation, however, as we have seen, the radical politics of her parents and the political climate of her country bar her from this crucial area of functioning. Her abandonment by Yvonne constitutes one of the cruelest scenes in the film. It is especially cruel because it is so poorly understood by Molly herself and because the defection has nothing to do with her. It is a direct result of her parents' opinions, decisions, and acts, with which the audience of the film is in sympathy, thus creating a genuine ethical dilemma. Molly's classmates snub her and exclude her from their company, and Yvonne, who initially defends her, fails in the end to remain loyal.

Meanwhile, Molly's parents, who have unwittingly caused this state of affairs in their daughter's life, have, as we know, deserted her as well. In addition, she is being betrayed by her own body, which is now rapidly changing. We see her several times studying herself in the mirror and powdering her face with makeup belonging to her imprisoned mother. Is she wondering who she really is and who she will become? Wondering, like young Emily, in Thornton Wilder's *Our Town*, whether she is pretty but with no mother there to assure her she is pretty enough for all normal purposes? Wondering how like and different she will be from her mother and what she will do someday? We see her proudly showing off her new, grown-up hairdo to Elsie for approval. In preadolescence, girls benefit greatly from close contact with one another and with various encouraging adults so as to feel reassured about the physical, as well as the psychological, changes they are undergoing. We recall the images of Annie John and her schoolmates congregating in the cemetery to display their changing bodies to one another, seeking solidarity. For Molly, parentless under apartheid in South Africa, the expectable quantum of loneliness and disorientation becomes extreme.

There is also, of course, an intense curiosity and embarrassment about adult sexual relations in pre- and early adolescence, a theme captured by the film in several scenes. In the absence of both parents and in their absence from each other, Molly sits down at the piano and imagines them dancing romantically together. By means of this fantasy, she retrieves the model she so badly craves, an image of the intactness of the parental couple.

Early on in the film, before she is imprisoned, Diana hosts a forbidden, illegal biracial party for her activist friends, a party that, incidentally, is raided by the police. Molly and Yvonne are in attendance. Watching and whispering, the two girls sip from glasses of wine. Just before the raid, the camera, panning the guests, zooms in on a black and white couple kissing. Embarrassed, Molly tries to hide this illicit behavior from Yvonne by holding up her wineglass as a shield before her friend's eyes. We can observe here how a typical preadolescent moment of sheepishness in the face of adult erotic behavior is exacerbated by the political climate, explicitly by the laws of apartheid, which had made this an unlawful act. Molly's shame is doubled, and she is especially uncomfortable because this is happening at her house in front of her best friend, who comes from a conservative family and, although neither she nor Yvonne yet knows it, will forsake her later on. Yvonne, by the way, who has apparently not yet been fully indoctrinated, seems far more curious and prurient than shocked.

School occasionally creates problems for young people of Molly's age as they begin to challenge the bases for what may have been, in their earlier years, a relatively benign, unquestioning respect for the older generation and its rules. New, more rebellious, and oppositional postures appear. Once again, *A World Apart* shows us how extreme political conditions complicate the normal state of affairs.

Molly refuses one day in school to sing the national anthem. This occurs immediately after the Special Branch South African police have invaded and searched her home. She squirms, moreover, in the presence of the headmistress of her school, who treats her with superficial solicitousness but whom Molly sees as a spineless representative of the oppressive regime that has victimized her family. To Molly, this woman is untrustworthy and potentially treacherous. We see her through Molly's eyes, even when she is trying to be kind, but, with our external perspective, we can also understand—as Molly cannot—that she, for her part, is operating under a system of tyranny that handicaps and constrains her as well. The scene recalls others we have witnessed, Mendel and Ludo and Annie, who each feel, in turn, alienated from and misunderstood by their teachers.

Molly stares absentmindedly out the window one day in school, and, pointedly, she refuses to listen when one of her teachers patriotically intones the glorious history of South Africa. With a mother in jail and a father gone underground, her mood and reaction are not hard to fathom, but the teacher interrupts the ideological monologue to ask spitefully:

"Are you with us, Molly?"

Molly does not answer, and another student, emboldened by the teacher's maliciousness, breaks the ensuing silence. Answering in Molly's place, this student responds, vindictively:

"No, she's against us."

This moment thus reduces all the ethical and psychological ambiguities to yet another stark dualism: *for* or *against,* as in *white* or *black, good* or *bad.* Such a confrontation in the classroom typifies the rhetorical strategies of all tyranny, which is to close off thought by labeling groups and condemning some while overidealizing others. Fortunately or unfortunately, after one has done that, one no longer has any need to think. One is freed from doubt, liberated from the weight of anxiety. By permitting her student to denounce Molly in this insolent manner, by egging her on in fact to do so, the classroom teacher acquiesces in the strategies of tyranny; thus, the short scene demonstrates that, in such a school, Molly cannot feel safe.

An especially valuable strategy of *A World Apart* for our study of parent-child relations is its brilliant twinning of Diana and Molly. Mother and daughter are, in a variety of ways, subtly paired, so that when something happens to Diana, something similar occurs in Molly's life. Diana's world, in other words, is actually mirrored in that of her eldest daughter. Whereas the audience viewing the film may partially discern this phenomenon so that it creates a strong sense of dramatic irony, it remains obscure to the characters themselves.

Shortly after the police raid their home and verbally assault Diana, Molly's former school friends insult her and call her a traitor. In both of these instances of attack, the aggression comes without warning and finds its victims unprepared. In a later set of paired scenes, just after Diana has been interrogated yet again in prison and is beginning—after an initial period of great courage and sangfroid—to experience the desperateness of her situation and her aloneness, Molly is shown being abandoned by Yvonne, who goes off after school that day with another girl, leaving Molly heartbroken.

In yet a third set of paired scenes, egregious male violence against both mother and daughter is portrayed. One of the most brutal of Diana's interrogators in jail slaps her roughly in the face when she refers accusatorily to his heinous crimes at Sharpeville. Similarly, as we have seen, Molly is verbally abused, threatened, and chased by Yvonne's racist father in his car as she runs in terror to escape him after trying to pay a visit to his daughter.

Throughout the story, Molly suffers for her mother's moral choices without fully understanding them and without having any opportunity to make up her own mind as to whether she concurs with them or not. It is very important to say, at this point, that Diana is portrayed as taking no time to try to explain anything to the girl, and one wonders whether her total abdication in this regard is absolutely necessary. Looking at it from the mother's point of view, she seems to feel that to begin to explain would have been to open the door to questions that could not be answered and that silence was, therefore, preferable to half-truths and frustration, although, of course, that is precisely the state of affairs created by the silence. In reflecting this way, we may recall the portrayals in Rosler's *Mendel* and Grossman's *See Under: LOVE*, where, likewise, the answers to children's questions seem to spawn further questions that become—for very different reasons—increasingly unanswerable.

What Slovo's film makes strikingly clear is that, unlike children, adults are expected to accept the consequences of their moral choices precisely because they are the ones choosing and because, presumably, they are counting with some measure of conviction on the potential long-range benefits to society of their choices. Children have no such opportunity to elect and no such comparable vision of the future. They therefore do not feel strengthened and ennobled by deprivation. They, like Molly, are vulnerable to hurt and confusion. They may be depressed by their parents' behavior, even when that behavior is directed toward social change that will one day be of benefit to them. Parenthetically, the young actress who plays Molly in the film conveys her depressive affect by inclining her head and dropping her shoulders. What empowers Diana—her fierce commitment, her belief in the rectitude of her cause, her willingness to sacrifice for it, and her trust in the future efficacy of her acts—works on her daughter Molly in exactly the opposite way.

We see this most clearly when Diana is arrested and is being led forcibly away from the house by the goons who have come for her. Molly cries out in a broken voice:

"Please don't go, Mommy!"

Notice the precise choice of words. By pleading with Diana not to go, Molly, in this moment of parting, shows that, like a small child, she still imbues her mother with the power not to go. But Diana Roth cannot "not go." She has no choice. She has no power. She is being *compelled* to go. Molly, however, continues to see her as an omnipotent mother, as *her* mother. And she desperately needs Diana to be strong, not only because of her own developmental requirements but because she is suffering and has only this one parent left to cling to. It is impossible for her to accept the reality, namely, that her tough-minded mother has been reduced to a victim and is at the mercy of the hated and feared police. Molly does not say, "I won't let you go." She does not address the police and beg, "Don't take my mommy away." She pleads with Diana to stay. This utterance all by itself, in its terrible poignancy, betrays her helplessness—her unmet needs, her loss. Her anxiety overwhelms any other possible mode of awareness or functioning. Watching her, listening to her sobs, we are brought into the scene with her and made to relive all the partings we have endured in our own lives.

Let's consider, in the final section of this chapter, the notion of the word *apart* and its ambiguities. In the beginning of the film, Diana clearly feels she is a part of something significant—a great movement with freedom and racial equality as its goal. Her mission energizes her. She is at one with it. Furthermore, she sees herself as carrying on the work of her husband, Gus Roth, a passionate, effective revolutionary. She and he are living apart during the time recorded by the film, but they are also a part of the worldwide Communist movement. In prison, when Diana finally breaks down under pressure and attempts suicide, she writes in her suicide note that she cannot let Gus down. The suicide, in other words, would prevent her from breaking down under torture and betraying him by revealing secrets that would harm others and their cause.

Yet she is also a part of a family—the mother of children. Who would be left to care for and raise these children if she honors her commitment to her husband and all that they have fought for? We discern levels of complexity here, for although on a manifest level Diana seems to indicate that her relationship with her absent husband and their comrades trumps her motherly love, this can only be a part of the story. Does being *a part* of one thing imply being *apart* from something else? Is this dichotomous thinking not simply another form of the rhetoric of tyranny?

In real life, Ruth First's own parents, Tilly and Julius First, were radical socialists from Latvia and Lithuania, respectively, and, as the character of the grandmother in the film reveals, they were deeply committed to the values they had passed on to their daughter. Thus, Diana's moral choice in attempting to take her own life would not have been inconsistent with what had been espoused in Ruth First's actual birth family. Even as such, however, the act seems unjustifiable. What does it mean that Diana shows herself ready to die in order that others may not die on her account and that she is ready to honor her pledge to her husband and place these moral imperatives on a higher plane than her obligation to her three young children? What kind of a mother is this? Interestingly, her act is not portrayed in the film as one of uncomplicated heroism and martyrdom. It is portrayed as a complex gesture compounded of enervation, desperation, cowardice, shame, and even guts and shrewd calculation.

For, although Diana is reviled by the police for having broken down under pressure, they immediately attend to her on that account. When they realize her life is in actual danger, they proceed without hesitation to save her, and they subsequently release her from prison to house arrest. Is there any sense in which she could have predicted and counted rashly and desperately on this?

Why, in fact, do the police save her life? Why is Diana sent home after her suicide attempt? I would suggest it is obviously because she is both a woman and white. Never, under such circumstances, would they have released a black man or a white man or a black woman. Her jailors, as I read the film, want her to submit, to give in. What they want, beyond any specific information, is to degrade and humiliate her, not to destroy her. They ask her, for example, at one point, whether she misses her children [*sic*]. Of course, at that moment, we might think of Elsie, who, while Diana is locked in prison being asked whether she misses her children, is similarly locked, in a way, in the prison of Diana's house caring for Diana's children and missing her own children. Apartheid keeps mothers and children apart.

The police taunt Diana:

"All this playing Joan of Arc is only an excuse for being a terrible mother," they say. And later:

"You've wasted your life; you could have done so much."

What incenses her male interrogators, it seems to me, is her courage, her defiance. Once she has broken down, they are able to finish with her and let her go. And we have a confluence of feminist and racial issues, for Diana, as a white woman, has had unique privileges accorded her. With regard to the black male prisoners, there was no quarter: they were, without mercy, maimed and murdered. This contrast is made explicit in the film when Elsie's brother Solomon is tortured before our eyes.

Ultimately, under apartheid, no one was exempt from suffering. Even those who thought they were gaining lost. *A World Apart* captures, under a cinematic microscope as it were, the ways this inhumane ideology deformed one mother-daughter dyad in a family that was struggling to change its society for the better while maintaining itself as an intact unit of that society and how that project became increasingly untenable. The final breakdown of the mother in prison can be regarded as symbolic of the family's failure as a whole to remain undivided under the impact of external centrifugal forces. We might see an analogy here to the situation of the family of Ludovic Fabre, similarly fighting a battle, albeit on very different grounds, in Berliner's film *Ma vie en rose,* with the larger sociocultural milieu in which it exists.

What matters to us here and now is that Slovo's 1988 film presents an extreme case of a situation from which none of us is exempt, a situation with which none of us is entirely unfamiliar. Its moral choices are not apart from our own. What kind of mothers, fathers, and children are we, and how do we balance the weights of our own manifold responsibilities? How well do we fathom the impact of our acts and decisions, even of those we take to be noble and good, on those we love? By what criteria and what scales of measurement shall we judge the far-reaching impact of the choices we make on those closest to us?

These are questions that, explored sensitively here in this film, extend in relevance far beyond the boundaries of South Africa and beyond the mise-en-scène of Shawn Slovo's evocative and profoundly disquieting work.

In My Mother's House

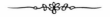

Mama, it is a play that tells the truth about people . . . I hope
it will make you very proud.

—LORRAINE HANSBERRY (LETTER TO HER MOTHER)

orraine Hansberry's 1959 play, *A Raisin in the Sun,* was both her
first and the first by any playwright of color to astonish Broadway.
Crossing boundaries of race, ideology, and class, it puts onstage an unforgettable portrayal of parent-child relations, bridging all gaps, and
the maturity of Hansberry's grasp, at the age of twenty-eight, is breath-
taking.

Staging her story of an African American family caught in webs of
bigotry and xenophobia, Hansberry takes us to postwar South Side
Chicago. Her larger social themes come to life through renderings of
parents and children who spar with and sustain one another across
three generations. These intergenerational exchanges are my focus.
Scenes that reveal gaps in understanding even when love is abiding
and strong. Scenes that show how children long for what parents can
neither comprehend nor give. Scenes that teach how sympathy and
identification falter but maintain themselves across gender and gener-
ational fault lines. Scenes that demonstrate how, by the end, one family manages to remain intact while trapped unavoidably by the residues
of slavery and vulnerable to ongoing affliction. This is a play from

which we can learn much we have not yet learned and much we badly need to learn.

Although *Raisin* belongs to the luminous first circle of mid-twentieth-century American drama, which includes *A Streetcar Named Desire* (1947), *Death of a Salesman* (1949), and *Long Day's Journey into Night* (1956), and although it may therefore be familiar, I would like to recall that the story begins with the bereaved Younger family awaiting a life insurance check that promises to ameliorate its situation. Each family member cherishes a dream of what might be done with the money. Lena (or Mama), the widow to whom the check belongs, is hoping to move them all out of their cramped rental quarters and buy a house and garden where her children can spread out and yet remain—significantly—under her roof.

Unlike film, where cameras rove while a story unfolds, staged plays depend strategically on the power of their discrete scenes. Each scene, one might say, counts as a fundamental unit of the dramatic art. In momentous scenes, two or more people interact, and their interchange is fraught with risk as it doubles in the provenance of live theater, which simultaneously presents living actors and imaginary characters so that every iteration of a scene is unique. *A Raisin in the Sun* unfurls its scenes in a dazzling progression like a parade. Or like a fireworks display in which each burst of glittering color outdoes the one that has just fallen from the sky.

Take act 1, scene 1, where, in a single stroke, an interchange epitomizes the drama to come and lays bare its psychological core. The curtain rises Friday morning on a cramped, overcrowded apartment, home to five members of the Younger family. Ten-year-old Travis sleeps on a fold-up couch in the living room. An improvised kitchen fills another corner. Wakened for school by his mother, Ruth, the boy is given his breakfast and then departs, as does his father, Walter Lee, Lena's thirty-five-year-old son, who works as a chauffeur. Lena now enters and seats herself while her daughter-in-law Ruth stands nearby, ironing. Unbeknownst yet to anyone else in the family, Ruth is newly pregnant. Lena's other child is her daughter Beneatha, a twenty-year-old college student, who saucily waltzes onstage from the bathroom her family shares with its neighbors.

Greeting the morning, her clever, high-strung, impressionable head spinning with new ideas, Beneatha informs Mama and Ruth that she is about to start guitar lessons in order to "express" herself and that she will *not* marry her apparent beau, the wealthy but "shallow" George Murchison. She is going to be a doctor, she adds, and, finally, she states offhandedly that none of this has anything to do with God. Mama warns her sternly against blasphemy, but Beneatha, bursting with youthful exuberance and sangfroid, prolongs her turgid rant on human independence:

"God," she declares airily, "is just one idea I don't accept."

Mama remains ominously silent. When Beneatha winds down, Mama rises heavily from her chair. Slowly and deliberately, she makes her way across the stage and, without a word, slaps Beneatha hard across the face.

"Now you say after me," she commands, "In my mother's house there is still God. [And she repeats] In my mother's house there is still God."   •

To cringe, to reel, to be stricken by the immense power that crouches, springs, and smites in this scene, one requires no belief in God nor any religious sentiments whatever. The interaction holds. It holds because this confrontation between Beneatha and Mama reanimates both onstage and offstage the most primordial human hierarchy we experience, namely, the preeminence of our mothers when we are small. As one five-year-old put it to her mommy, "I love you best because you had me inside you from the beginning." Love. Fear. Power. Even, seemingly, over birth and death. Mothers know it. Think of Clytemnestra, queen of Argos, who shamelessly uses it when she faces her murderous son in Aeschylus's *Oresteia*. Not content with the slap, Mama reminds Beneatha with crystalline clarity just who stands at the head of her family.

Puissant, matriarchal, Mama makes the decisions. The house all five of them inhabit is hers; the ten thousand dollars of life insurance money is hers. Founded in love, tempered by generosity, her dominion is absolute. Guiding and providing, she does so not only as mother, mother-in-law, and grandmother but in lieu of her deceased husband whose role and mantle she has assumed. She listens "vigorously," as Hansberry tells us, to everybody's phone calls. Beneatha, at one point, calls her a tyrant.

Yet Lena Younger knows fretfully that her two feisty adult children submit but restively to her will. Her fate will be to come to terms with this fact and to acknowledge the fallout from her all-embracing love. Such learning comes hard. Especially when resisted by a hostile world that has squeezed her family all too tightly together. Like the scrawny potted plant she nourishes, her children have insufficient space in which to spread their leaves and branches. They need to reach upward toward the sun. Yet Lena Younger seems only superficially able to affirm their adulthood. Even by the end of *A Raisin in the Sun,* her acceptance of Walter Lee's and Beneatha's maturity seems incomplete. What makes mothers, to a greater or lesser extent, deny and oppose their children's needs to grow up?

It is a truth nobody likes to confess. Yet, as philosophers, notably, Georg Wilhelm Friedrich Hegel and Martin Buber, have argued in their respective analyses, every form of recognition entails a dependency on the subjectivity of another. Children's love and respect make their mothers and fathers feel like parents, not the biological facts of birth or the legal facts of adoption. (Who, apropos, can forget the thrill of a baby's first truly responsive smile?) In this fundamental sense, if in no other, a mother and a father are forever dependent. When the slave escapes from bondage, when the student ceases to pay attention, when the child runs away from home, what becomes of master, teacher, or parent?

But we can go further. For, beyond these fundamental relations of recognition, power, and knowledge, a mother who has brought up a child is forever barred from seeing that child as a stranger. To a stranger, you are more or less whoever you appear to be in your present incarnation. Not to your mother. To her, you are a painted palimpsest of overlays, scrims, and veneers; you are all the previous children you have been in the past—smiling, creeping, toddling, falling, climbing, vanishing, returning, failing, achieving—from the moment of your birth. For your mother, historical perspective supervenes. Yet children—like Beneatha and Walter Lee—come to a point where they crave the opposite. They need to break free of the past. They need to be seen and dealt with by their mothers as they are in the present alone. From this discrepancy between the wish to escape history on the one side and the inescapability of history on the other comes much of the psychological dynamism of Hansberry's play.

In terms of the uses and abuses of history for life (to borrow the title of Friedrich Nietzsche's 1874 essay where he ponders these problems, though not psychologically), it is important to note that history actually does matter on the child's side as well. Especially in adulthood, when we can look back over the years of our parents' lives that we shared with them. Stricken feelings may ensue. This was true in my own life when my aged father suffered from kidney failure and was taken regularly for dialysis. The nurses saw him not as the magisterial gentleman I knew him to be but as a wizened old man. How I agonized over this discrepancy and wept because I knew there was no way of correcting their perceptions. Thus, in Hansberry's play, we see a mother who is immersed in history yet tries to move on versus her adult children who feel oppressed by that same history and sense that only by setting it aside—at least temporarily—will they be able to evolve.

Before putting her onstage, Hansberry describes Mama in regal terms, with "noble bearing . . . rather as if she imagines that as she walks she still bears a basket or a vessel on her head." We know her right away. She radiates an atavistic splendor. She is an eminence from the wellsprings of childhood fantasy. Exceeding all categories of race, class, epoch, and site, she radiates the saturated colors of inalienable psychological verisimilitude. For such a mother to give up her children—in any way, at any time—would be unimaginable. Think of Maria Theresa, the grand Habsburg empress of Austria and Hungary, who sent her daughter Marie Antoinette off to marry the dauphin in France but not without spies installed at Versailles to report back every detail of the girl's daily activities to her faraway but ever watchful mother (Cranshaw 1969). A Holocaust survivor, sent abroad by *Kindertransport*, told me how her mother's letters followed her across the ocean like hands holding on to her from afar (Lore Segal, personal communication, October 2009). Recently, in a penciled diary shared with me by a childhood friend, I found an entry detailing a young mother's "physical feeling of loss" when her five year old went off to kindergarten. The child's absence caused such privation that the mother underwent a kind of mourning. Similarly, when my own first child left home, I telephoned my father to bemoan my loss. With impeccable logic, he pointed out the splendid opportunities that awaited her and told me how uncomplicatedly pleased I should feel. But mothers—queens and otherwise—hold tight. In Mama's case, being without her husband exacerbates her tenaciousness. She has habits of orchestration she herself half sees. As she protests, in self-betrayal, to her daughter-in-law, "I ain't meddling."

Perhaps not unexpectedly, Mama's hierarchical stance echoes in Walter Lee's relations with his wife, Ruth, who, though displaced as the "woman of the house" by her mother-in-law, imitates her by failing to differentiate at times between husband and son. Ruth's manner of awakening Travis and Walter Lee and hustling them along sounds strikingly similar. She talks to them with the same tone, thus unwittingly perpetuating Mama's infantilizing behavior. When Travis asks Ruth for fifty cents to bring to school, she refuses. They don't have it. Boy and mother tussle a few minutes, Travis wheedling, Ruth resisting. Then Walter Lee enters. Overhearing them, he feels ashamed at not being able to provide his boy with such a small sum of money (money being the symbol of power), and so, in defiance of Ruth's "no," he gives Travis his own carfare money and a bit more besides—an act of generosity and solidarity with his son but also of rebellion against maternal authority. Ruth, as Hansberry writes, now has "murder in her eyes." Travis, bonding with his daddy, goes happily off to school with his fifty cents. Later Walter Lee realizes he cannot get to work without the carfare he has just given to Travis, and he is obliged to ask for it from Ruth (again, qua mother), who hands it to him with no comment.

Such parallels occur verbally as well as behaviorally. In the same scene, Mama laments to Ruth that something has come down between her and her children that doesn't let them understand each other, and she doesn't know what it is. Walter Lee echoes these sentiments almost verbatim in the second act when he opines to Ruth that something has come down between them. And Ruth herself uses a similar phrase to describe her own troubles when she tells Mama that something is happening between Walter and herself and she doesn't know what it is. Thus, a ripple effect occurs when adult children are not permitted to function independently. Later Mama intervenes to make Walter Lee listen to his wife tell about her new pregnancy. He objects to her interference and points out that he is a grown man. Mama, however, replies that he is still in her house and her presence. Thus, the hierarchy stands.

How should we interpret these scenes and the visceral stamina and obduracy that characterize their intergenerational divides? Like walls of brick, they cannot be felled by huffing and puffing, no matter how clever the wolf. Mama digs in and roots herself intransigently within her own perspective, rather like a stationary artist who draws the model by positioning an easel in the same spot every day while her child moves around to the other side of the model's stand. Might it not be possible for a parent to circle around the model's stand and try to see from another side—from the child's perspective—while continuing to hold fast to her own perceptual center? How invested must each member of the dyad be in an oppositional point of view in order to act and not be paralyzed by ambivalence? For paralysis can be a consequence of giving up a unilateral perspective. We observe this in Tolstoy's *War and Peace* when Nikolai Rostov, who has intended to rush into battle and cut down the enemy, finds himself positioned at last so as to be able to kill a Napoleonic soldier but realizes he is unable to do so because, when he looks at the Frenchman, he sees not the face of an enemy but simply that of a boy. Our ability to change places with each other mentally—to move around the model's stand or scale the wall that divides us—might stay our hands or voices from acts of aggression. Seeing from the other side might even improve the chances for human survival. Rather than producing a hesitant intellect (which in itself might not be so terrible), such imaginative action could well enable us to take more of "the whole field into consideration" (William James 1899).

A Raisin in the Sun offers a playground in which to experiment with such ideas. Reading it, watching it, thinking about its characters, loving them, trying to get inside them, we find ourselves inventing happier, less conflictual scenarios: revolving model's stands in artists' studios, perhaps, or walls of latticework instead of brick, or hedgerows, so that people can peek through, touch hands, and try to understand one another instead of shutting each other out.

Mama, in one glorious moment of rapport, does overcome her unitary perspective. This occurs in act 2, scene 2. Beneatha has been out on a date with the previously mentioned "shallow" George Murchison, who hails from a well-heeled family with conventional ideas. Smitten with Beneatha, George Murchison expects her, as his chosen girlfriend, to be grateful for his attentions and to emulate his style and values. Rebellious and ruggedly independent, as we have seen, Beneatha will have none of it. George tries to kiss her while they sit together on the sofa and is piqued when she rebuffs him. Making matters worse, he harangues her with sexist propaganda and then leaves in a huff, bidding a fast good night to Mama, who has just entered with some packages.

Immediately sensing the tension, Mama shrewdly asks Beneatha whether she and George had a nice time together. When Beneatha retorts "no" in a sullen voice, Mama, after asking her why, actually listens to her answer:

"Mama, George is a fool, honest."

At this point, Lena might easily choose to make some palliative remark, object, or ask her daughter to be more charitable, in short, take George Murchison's part. What she does, however, is none of the above. She accepts Beneatha's words at face value. She gets it right. First, however, just to make sure, she asks and gets the same deadpan reply. After that, in an inspired moment, Mama pronounces:

"Well, I guess you better not waste your time with no fools."

Another stunning moment in the play. Followed by a long pause. Mama puts her groceries away, and Beneatha gets ready, slowly, to leave the room. Before going, she turns back, casts a loving eye on her mother, and thanks her. When Mama asks why, Beneatha explains:

"For understanding me this time."

A gladsome exchange: catching that invisible ball and throwing it back in perfect synchrony.

But how does it happen? Mama's relationship with Beneatha, we can't help noticing, seems to play out differently from the one she has with her son. She slaps her daughter, as we have seen, and disciplines her. Yet Beneatha goes right on rebelling. She refuses to back down. It is exactly this sparring, this frank back-and-forth between them that, I suggest, enables Mama to learn, grow, and change gradually in her relations with Beneatha. Opposition can force us—if we survive it—to achieve new levels of growth. With her son Walter Lee, Mama cannot interact the same way. She cannot lay down the law to him as she can with Beneatha. She protects and coddles him as she does Travis. He, in turn, respecting her, never—despite his frustration and resentment—openly fights her. Consequently, there is no comparable learning curve in their relationship, and it is he, far more than Beneatha, who feels profoundly misunderstood and oppressed. In part, the reason Mama gets it right with Beneatha, at least this time, is that Beneatha has fought her, and Mama, even when she fails to grasp the nuances, identifies strongly with that defiant spirit, so similar to her own.

Let's turn now to Walter Lee, who, in the opening scene, tells us with fierce passion how disempowered he is. His job as chauffeur to a white man accords him no sense of accomplishment or scope. It demeans him. Furthermore, he cannot earn enough to strike out on his own. Meanwhile, living under his mother's roof replicates this constellation. Chaffing and irascible, he speaks of his dreams. He yearns to emancipate himself from the oppression he feels on all sides. Bitterly, he protests that he is thirty-five years old, has been married eleven years, and has a son who sleeps in the living room. He opens and closes car doors and drives a white man around in a limousine. The future, he feels, is:

"Hanging over there at the edge of my days. Just waiting for me—a big looming blank space—full of *nothing*. Just waiting for *me*."

The only grown man in a house full of women, Walter Lee craves comradeship. Falling in with a few disreputable cronies, he plans to open a liquor store with them and entrusts one of them with the insurance money destined for Beneatha's medical school tuition. Soon he finds himself betrayed. Morally, the betrayal is the thief's, yet Walter Lee's judgment is to blame. By basing emancipation on his mother's largesse, he perpetuates an important element of the very dependency from which he seeks to free himself. Moreover, the intensity of his wish to escape pushes him to ignore in his buddy the unsavory side that is patent from the start to both his wife and his sister. In Ruth's words from the opening scene, "Willy Harris [the thief] is a good-for-nothing . . ." Walter Lee, however, annuls this judgment by responding simply that nobody in his family understands him.

Ultimately, the climactic scene of *A Raisin in the Sun,* goes to him. It is a victory that, although we know it to be pyrrhic, nevertheless makes our hearts soar with joy. Another great dramatic scene and one that forms a bookend with the one I described first between Beneatha and Mama. Walter Lee confronts a sniveling racist, Karl Lindner, who has come to bully and bribe the Younger family with cash to stay out of the house Mama has by now purchased for them with the rest of the insurance money. The house, needless to say, is located in an all white neighborhood. Proudly and with dignity, Walter Lee informs Lindner, representative of the "New Neighbors Orientation Committee," that his family will be not be intimidated. His father, he says proudly, has earned that house for them "brick by brick."

Pronouncing these fateful words, Walter Lee holds Travis in front of him. Having already presented the boy as his son, he positions himself, as it were, between past and future, between his deceased father and his growing son. This way, in the last moments of the play, Walter Lee reclaims his dignity and a measure of his long-aspired freedom. Hearing his speech but not seeing it (she closes her eyes from too much emotion), Mama comprehends its significance, not just for the family but for him. "He finally come into his manhood today, didn't he?" she marvels, "Kind of like a rainbow after the rain . . ."

But *why* does Walter Lee do this? What makes him change his mind at the last minute and defend his mother's choice to buy a house in racist Clybourne Park? After all, when he first learns that Lindner will be coming to bribe them with money in order to keep them out, he is ready to accept the bribe and even to stage a Jim Crow performance to cinch the deal. Since Willy Harris made off with thousands of their dollars, Walter Lee views the bribe as a way of recovering a portion of it. What makes him change course and act heroically?

The minute he announces his intention to capitulate, Beneatha expresses her contempt. She calls him a "toothless rat." This is an image that has reappeared several times already as a symbol for everything the family yearns to leave behind. Mama has agreed with Ruth to call their present living quarters a "rat trap," and, later on, in a scene many stage productions have excised, Travis goes out to play and returns from the street with a sadistic description of how he and some friends have just tortured a live rat. Not content with her insult, Beneatha renounces Walter Lee as her brother. Hansberry at this point gives Mama one of her most moving speeches. Turning to her daughter, she asks:

"Child, when do you think is the time to love somebody the most? When they done good and made things easy for everybody? Well then, you ain't through learning—because that ain't the time at all. It's when he's at his lowest and can't believe in hisself 'cause the world done whipped him so."

This lesson comes hard and not just to Beneatha. How can we find it in our hearts to love one another when both we and they are unlovable? Walter Lee pays attention.

A moment later, the door opens and Lindner walks in with his briefcase filled with papers. Travis is present. Ruth, fearing her husband will capitulate and accept the scoundrel's offer, immediately sends the child away. Mama intervenes. Looking straight into Walter Lee's eyes, she addresses not him but her grandson, Travis, and she tells him to stay right where he is. To Walter Lee, she charges:

"And you make him understand what you are doing, Walter Lee. You teach him good. Like Willy Harris taught you. You show where our five generations done come to. Go ahead son—Go ahead."

It is with this combination of sibling rejection and maternal dare that Walter Lee goes forward to refuse the offer. But is he merely shamed and bullied into it? I think not. True, Mama has not been gentle, but, as always, she is crystal clear. My view is that she appeals to Walter Lee as a *father*. Implicitly, she draws a sharp line between him and the corrupt Willy Harris. Whatever Walter Lee does right now, she makes him see, will be his lesson to his son. And, as we know, Walter Lee cares deeply for Travis. What kind of lesson, Mama asks him, does he want to teach his boy? In this way, she gives him a leg up and helps him scale the wall. She encourages him to switch from being principally a child ("Ain't nobody with me!" he had cried earlier, "Not even my own mother!") to being a mature adult who is the father of his own son. It is this, I believe, that causes Walter Lee to swerve, rise, and take a commanding position. Mama has shown him a new primary way to be, and, tacitly, we know that Ruth is pregnant so there may be another child for him to father as well. *It is as a father that Walter Lee speaks his "no."* He accomplishes it with eloquence and simplicity.

He tells Lindner they don't want his money, and then, as Hansberry notes tersely in her stage directions, he "turns and walks away."

By helping someone find a new primary way to be himself or herself, we stimulate in that person an alternate repertoire of behavior. Whatever happens now, Walter Lee has claimed his moment. His son witnessed it. As did his wife, sister, and mother. It is a moment that will not be forgotten.

Let's turn now to Ruth, who is both mother and mother-to-be, a subtle character who rarely appears center stage. Parenthetically, one of Hansberry's gifts is to make us care deeply for her characters (with the exception, no doubt, of those few we despise as fully as we adore the others). Ruth appeals for her gentleness, sensitivity, and quiet strength and for her efforts to promote tranquil relations among members of the fiery family into which she married. Onstage during the scene when Mama slaps Beneatha, she remains mostly silent. When Mama leaves the room, however, and Beneatha, unrepentant, continues to mutter about tyranny never putting a God in the sky, Ruth goes over to the door behind which Mama has retired and calls through it that Beneatha says she's sorry. This is nothing more nor less than a prevarication aimed to heal the wound that has opened between parent and child.

Ruth goes on to ask Beneatha not to be nasty to her brother, and then, when Walter Lee counterattacks, she chides him on Beneatha's behalf. A peacemaker by choice and inclination, Ruth refrains from malice herself as we saw in the interchange with Walter Lee early in the morning when he sheepishly asks her for money after he has given all his cash to Travis; she supplies it without rancor. She reminds the rest of the family that the insurance money belongs exclusively to Mama and strives to modulate their strident voices. Yet she, too, wants desperately to leave, and when the moving men finally get there and Walter Lee has had his moment of glory, it is gentle Ruth who lets herself go in an explosion of relief and elation: "LET'S GET THE HELL OUT OF HERE!" she exclaims. Hansberry puts this into capital letters just to make sure the actress gets it right.

Well named, as others have surely noticed, Ruth, despite an occasional tiff with Mama, cannot help but remind us of Ruth in the Bible, who devotedly follows her Israelite mother-in-law Naomi from the land of Moab all the way to Bethlehem in Judah after their husbands have died and refuses to leave her. Ruth Younger cherishes, in Hansberry's play, a relationship with her mother-in-law that is similarly devoted. And just as Ruth, a gleaner, must hover at the edges of the field, so Ruth Younger moves and speaks at the margins of the play. Yet both Ruths possess extraordinary valor; both are also, interestingly, mothers to be.

As a demonstration of the love between Ruth and her mother-in-law, one amusing moment occurs when they are onstage fantasizing about the forthcoming check. Everyone has a practical goal: Walter Lee wants to invest in a liquor store; Beneatha wants to pay for medical school; Mama wants to make down payment on a house. Uniquely, it is Ruth who conceives a spectacularly impractical way to spend the money, a way with pleasurable consequences for Mama alone.

"You know what you should do, Miss Lena?" she proposes, "You should take yourself a trip somewhere. To Europe or South America or someplace . . . I'm serious," she goes on, warming to her fantasy. She tells Mama to pack up and leave and enjoy herself and forget about the family.

It's a genuine Ruth and Naomi moment in terms of the love and care that motivate it, and Mama of course pooh-poohs it. But it provides clues to Ruth's character, for, in wanting to imagine something wonderful for Mama, she betrays her own wishes to get away, see the world, and escape the humdrum existence that has ensnared her. As she says half jokingly to Walter Lee when he complains about his lot, she would rather be living in Buckingham Palace than on the South Side of Chicago. Another interpretation of this scene might be that Ruth wishes to get rid of Mama and give *herself* a holiday—in the sense of a respite from domination, interference, and "meddling." But this motive coexists easily with the first while remaining less conscious; the motives blend. When we are alert to them, they give us a fuller picture not only of Ruth's love for Mama but of what Ruth shares with her husband, for he, too, as we know, is a dreamer with high-flying wishes and plenty of gall simmering beneath.

Ruth, pregnant from the opening of the play (as we learn through Mama's shrewdness), visits an abortionist and even takes the fateful step of making a payment in advance. This seems an act that goes counter to all she holds dear. Mama tells Walter Lee about it, but he balks in disbelief. He says Mama doesn't know Ruth if she thinks Ruth would do that.

Of course she *has* done that and for a plenitude of understandable reasons: the unrelenting poverty of her family; the necessity to work as a domestic day servant to make ends meet; Beneatha's educational ambitions, which preclude her from contributing; Mama's advancing age; and the enormous drain a new baby would make on the entire family. These are the reasons Mama implies when she undeceives Walter Lee and tells him, "When the world gets ugly enough, a woman will do anything for her family. *The part that's already living.*"

Yet beneath this explanation lies, I suggest, another, namely, the faltering relationship within the marital couple. Walter Lee, through his dealings with the men who later prove false to him, forsakes Ruth emotionally. She complains that he brings these men into the living room at night—Bobo and Willy Harris—and talks with them in loud voices so that Travis cannot sleep. When she asks him to discuss this with her, he hurts her by saying he wants to talk with people who understand him.

Loving him but unable to reach him, Ruth feels she has lost her way of getting through. He, on the other side, feels she is incapable of sharing his dreams and that, like Mama, she seeks only to placate him with offers of food and drink—eggs, coffee, hot milk—as though he were an errant child.

This divide within the conjugal couple is what troubles Ruth most: the felt lack on both sides, at this critical juncture, of the special love that underpins an infant's sense of security in the world. Without the reassurance of enduring bonds, without intimate, mutual, sustaining adult relations, Ruth cannot go forward with a new pregnancy. She cannot do it alone. If Hansberry's character is—as I read her—a strong and subtle woman, it seems plausible that her visit to the abortionist can be read as a cri de coeur, an act both courageous and foolhardy at once (especially given the physical dangers of abortion in her time), not only a capitulation but a plea and a message.

More than a half century ago, Bruno Bettelheim (1950) published a controversial book in which he made use of the expression "love is not enough," and I'd like to borrow this phrase because it furnishes an important corollary to Mama's beautiful lesson to Beneatha that there is "*always* something left to love." Among members of the Younger family, we find no dearth of love. Even when brother and sister duel with words, even when Walter Lee simmers with alienation, even when Mama flares up, we know the default position in this family is love. Their problems are of understanding, not devotion. This is often so. Children rarely say "You don't love me," but frequently they complain "You don't understand." *A Raisin in the Sun* sounds this theme as a leitmotif. Its characters openly and consistently accuse one another of failing to understand.

Let's analyze several moments in the play when the words "you don't understand" are spoken. What can we learn from them?

The first mention occurs when Walter Lee accuses Ruth by saying that colored women don't know how to build their men up and make them feel important. His rhetorical strategy is to render his interlocutor incapable of self-defense by placing her into an ineluctable category. Predictably, Ruth throws up her hands and admits that since she is a colored woman she can't help herself. Walter Lee's accusation leaves her no choice but to opt out, and she does so without making any further efforts to understand him. The battle is over; Walter Lee wins, but his victory proves pyrrhic since what remains is exactly the same impasse as before, namely, that he still feels misunderstood.

Shortly thereafter, speaking to no one in particular but in the presence of both Ruth and Beneatha, Walter Lee exclaims that nobody in the house will ever understand him. Here the *ineluctable category* strategy remains in place, but Beneatha, who is rarely passive, picks up his gauntlet and tells her brother that no one understands him because he is "a nut." Denying the implication that she is too ignorant to understand him, she hurls back an insult of her own and labels him crazy. Now she is off the hook, for who can understand a nut? Once again, the original impasse is maintained but with added spite. After these exchanges, the characters involved immediately exit the stage. Thus, we see how "you don't understand" aborts communication just the way a red light stops traffic.

Beneatha, when the subject of George Murchison comes up, tries to explain to Mama and Ruth what she finds objectionable about him. Ruth fails to get what Beneatha means by "shallow," and Beneatha blurts out by way of retort that anyone who married her brother would never be able to understand. This enrages Mama, whose precious son is being maligned, and we notice how similar Beneatha's guilt by association is to the ineluctable category strategy used by Walter Lee. In this case, Ruth does not get angry, and the conversation continues, thereby giving Beneatha a chance to clarify why she feels she could never be serious about George Murchison. Toward the end of the scene, a new conflict flares up between Beneatha and Mama, but it has nothing to do with beaux at this point: God has upstaged George Murchison. What I read here is that, when the person accused of not understanding stays calm and neither surrenders nor counterattacks, the conversation may continue and even result in greater mutual comprehension. But Ruth is not Beneatha's mother.

Perhaps the most poignant accusation of misunderstanding occurs right after the insurance check arrives. Ruth has returned from the abortionist. Walter Lee is refusing to talk to her. Mama asks what is eating him. He tries to explain by describing his demoralizing job and ends by saying he doesn't know if he can make her understand. He continues to try, however. He details the prestige, independence, and happiness he thinks money will procure. Mama's response is to remind him of her childhood in the South. She tells him how worried they used to be about not getting lynched and how they tried to go north and about struggling to stay alive. She reminds him of his own childhood and how she and his dad kept him out of trouble till he was grown up.

Mama, of course, responds from a perspective steeped in history. She sees the present only in its relation to the past. Abjectly frustrated, Walter Lee just gives up. He strokes her hand and sighs:

"You just don't understand, Mama, you just don't understand."

What makes this so poignant is that Walter Lee craves affirmation. Mama, on the other hand, lives with what has come before. Their ways of seeing don't jibe. Each speaks the truth. Each possesses the authenticity of his or her unique perspective. Neither one can take "the whole field" into consideration. And the son's tender caress of his mother's hand reveals the truth of Bettelheim's phrase, "love is not enough." The gesture may remind us also of the ending of Kurt Tucholsky's poem "Mother's Hands," cited in the chapter "Pinches and Kisses" on *Annie John*, where adult children likewise stroke their aging mother's hands.

Later on, after Mama has made the down payment on the house, told her family about it, and seen how desperately Walter Lee needs a chance to do something his own way, she hands over the rest of the money to him. His crony Willy Harris, as we know, will eventually steal it. There is, however, a moment of high exultation when Walter Lee, believing in the imminent fulfillment of his dreams, gathers little Travis up in his arms and starts imagining a wonderful future that is somehow going to start "after tonight." When Travis asks him what he means ("What you gonna do tonight, Daddy?"), Walter Lee responds that the boy wouldn't understand yet. Once again, the curtain comes down after the "you wouldn't understand." But we sense something a little different. This time Walter Lee has added the crucial word *yet,* which opens a door to possible future understanding. Rather than saying "no" to his child, this parent is saying "not yet." As we know, there are good reasons why Walter Lee would not want to give precise details about a liquor store project to his ten year old. The phrase "you wouldn't understand" is couched here as a protection rather than an indictment. Even so, it retains its red light effect of shutting down further conversation.

A final instance differs from all the others. Here impasse is exactly what is required for the situation at hand. We are now at the very end of the play. Walter Lee has made his refusal speech to Lindner with Travis on hand and marched offstage. Lindner, all flustered and perturbed, his bribe money turned down, looks toward Mama as if she, the most senior member of the family, might countermand her son's decree and accept the bid to buy them out. Mama, who, over the course of the play, has been accused so many times by her children of not understanding, now turns majestically toward this unwelcome stranger. In a brilliant tour de force, she recognizes that *her* time has come. Addressing the man regally in a ringing reiteration of her children's words, she says, simply:

"I'm afraid you don't understand."

After this, there is nothing for the man to do but leave. It is a moment of perfect symmetry in which strands of psychological meaning come together. For, in this play, the phrase "you don't understand" has been used as an appeal, an accusation, a lament, a weapon, and a way—outstandingly—of closing the door.

Before closing the door ourselves, however, there is one important character I have not mentioned: Joseph Asagai, Beneatha's second and thoroughly appealing Nigerian beau. Not wishing to leave him out, I believe I have discovered a legitimate role for him that fits our theme, namely, that he can be read as a "way out" for Beneatha. What I mean is that, by opening her mind to a host of new possibilities, Asagai helps her to extricate herself from her family but without in any sense undermining its integrity and without failing to respect its deep and loyal ties. Asagai can also be read as a "way in," for he initiates Beneatha into

the discovery of her cultural and ethnic roots. He affirms and cele-
brates her career ambitions, her natural hairstyle, her ebullience, her
questioning stance toward life, her independence of thought, and her
rebelliousness. Importantly, he teaches her that reliance on her
mother (i.e., on the life insurance money) cannot and should not be
the only way to achieve her goals. He promotes her evolution.

In purely pragmatic terms, much is left unchanged by Hansberry's
final curtain. The Younger family is set to move out of its worn quarters
into a bright new home with more space and a garden for Mama's
plant, but the house will have been bought with Mama's insurance
money. Walter Lee will presumably continue working, at least for the
time being, as a chauffeur. Bigoted white neighbors will make efforts to
render the family's life unpleasant in their new neighborhood, even,
perhaps, dangerous. But what we have witnessed psychologically, in the
internal workings of the family, is, by the end of the play, a sea change
and pledge that henceforth greater understanding will prevail. Mama
has learned that she must share her authority; Walter Lee has proven,
to himself importantly, as well as to others, the extent of his moral
courage.

A Raisin in the Sun offers paradigms for psychological change that
lead well beyond its time and place. Indeed, when I think back over the
play as a whole, an image ricochets through my mind—a ball made of
rubber bands. Do you know what I mean? You pull a strand of it and try
to draw it away, but it bounces back. I see Mama at the center of this
ball, and all her children, including Ruth and Travis, as rubber bands
that keep pulling away and springing back. Eventually, a day comes
when the bands work loose from the core and form the beginnings of
new, separate balls of their own. Or they simply break. But the play
ends before anything like that happens. Externally, the home of the
Youngers is about to change, but psychologically it will still be Mama's
house, and the play makes us ruminate on how, in other families as
well, a centripetal maternal force can prove irresistible.

I am picturing one of the most striking visual artworks of our time:
a gargantuan spider called *Maman,* sculptured by Louise Bourgeois, a
huge creature wrought of bronze, stainless steel, and marble, a dark

Louise Bourgeois (1999), *Maman,* sculpture in mixed media. (Courtesy of Visual Artists and Galleries Association.)

monster that can spin a web, provide shelter, protect, and menace all at once and to which the artist has given the name "Mother." Visitors to the Tate Modern in London—or to the many other venues worldwide where incarnations of this work may be found—walk through her giant legs and sit under her. This *Maman* is a veritable house, tent, bridge, and cage, and Louise Bourgeois raises with her, in solid form, texture, and light and shadow, questions about the uncanny power of mothers that echo in the stirring scenes of Lorraine Hansberry's dramatic art, questions that fearless artists continue to dare to pose.

An Alien Child

Every child born into the world is nature's attempt to make a
perfect human being.
—THORNTON WILDER

Children are not born human . . .
—JACQUES BARZUN

Nothing in his touch or his look ever seemed to say, this is
my mother.
—DORIS LESSING

Almost from the start of her 1988 novel, *The Fifth Child*, Doris Lessing
makes her reader anxious. She arouses a level of discomfort that
crescendos as page after page is breathlessly turned. We are privy to the
story of a young couple who, in rebellion against the mores of their
era—England in the late 1960s—enact a redemptive fantasy by attempting to create an idyllic old-fashioned family. They produce four
children in rapid succession and, after relying on their compliant albeit
skeptical and aging parents for financial and other help, find themselves with a fifth child who is monstrous. This fifth child's presence
plunges the family into despair and blasts their dreams of happiness.

Lessing refuses to provide any answers for the questions she raises
about the risks and dangers of human reproduction, about *becoming*
parents as well as *being* parents, and about what happens when the

needs of one destructive child trump those of the rest of his family without affording any discernible benefits to him. She intends us to close her book, it appears, with even more anxiety than we had at first, but this may depend partly on our expectation of closure in works of art. Lessing has none to give.

What she does give calls forth our reserves of moral fortitude, for, by withholding comfort and denying us answers, she forces us to tolerate an unusually elevated level of ambiguity. We are not permitted to reduce this complexity to a binary system. Having called her work a classic horror story, she affords us an uneasy ride in which turbulence unseats us on every page, and we are plunged headlong into her story on the tracks of chilling, suspenseful prose. By the time we close the covers of *The Fifth Child*, we are emotionally drained, suspended in a state that includes irresolution and mourning.

We meet her young 1960s London couple as they are deploring what they judge to be the sexually permissive mores of their time. They reject their age-mates, who sleep around, and they are persuaded that having children is, by contrast, the answer. To revert to a traditional view of life lived in a long-term marriage under the roof of a capacious home filled with children and punctuated by large family gatherings on holidays is, they convince themselves, the way to escape the greed-ridden, sex-obsessed decade in which they are living.

We meet them, Harriet and David Lovatt, when they are still strangers to one another, just as they are to us, on page 1 of the novel. They are attending a boisterous office party at which they both feel like outsiders. Each of them hangs back in the midst of whirling, seductively garbed colleagues who pack the dance floor and seem to be undulating "on invisible turntables." Noticing each other, they meet and then leave the fray, and we follow at a discreet distance as they go off to talk quietly. At first, our inclination is to wish them well: after all, they seem so innocent, so admirable in their principled determination to buck the times. At twenty-four, Harriet is still, Lessing pointedly informs us, a virgin.

Sweeping the couple up, her breakneck narrative whips them along, and we go with them. No time to reflect. No time to pause.

Sprinting from sentence to sentence, outpaced by the velocity of their story, we almost fear we have accidentally skipped whole pages. Then, however, we turn back to look for what we think we've missed, and we realize we have read every word. By page 14, this couple, who met on page 1, have married, purchased a sprawling, oversized Victorian house they can ill afford—a house with a neglected garden—in suburban London, and are pregnant with their first child. Significantly, they have borrowed money from David's father to pay for their mortgage. As one child after another arrives, Harriet's overworked mother, Dorothy, is conscripted to help. Uncomplaining but incredulous, she appears, and while Harriet nurses each newborn she cares for the rest.

Lingering for a moment over this narrative pace, I want to suggest that Lessing mirrors here the actual lived pace of many young parents who, preoccupied with practical affairs, race through the early years of their children's lives only to awaken one day and find that the era has fled. There has been insufficient reflection, insufficient time to ask why.

Our initial sympathy for the couple begins to falter. Harriet and David, who first seemed appealing in their principled boycott of the sex-crazed sixties, begin, little by little, to display an eerie self-absorption and monomaniacal intransigence. Their fantasy of ideal family life depends increasingly on the largesse of others whose generosity they take for granted. Dismissing their parents' gentle protests, health worries, and purse strings, they fail to notice that the project is causing increasing problems for themselves as well. Exhausted by her nearly perpetual state of pregnancy and lactation, Harriet grows irritable toward her brood of children and snaps at them when they demand attention. She and David experience, symptomatically, what Lessing calls a "half guilt," which I take to mean a half-disavowed guilt, one acknowledged but not taken seriously, and Harriet—in response to the stated and unstated criticism of others—begins to refer to herself, somewhat ironically, as a "criminal," one, that is, who goes against the mores of society.

Among ill omens ignored is the birth, early on, to one of Harriet's sisters (who is unhappily married) of a Down syndrome child called Amy, a birth Harriet glibly explains as a consequence of the couple's strained relations. She and David, implicitly, on the other hand, since they have good marital relations, can blithely continue their ever-expanding reproductive plans.

By the advent of Harriet's disastrous fifth pregnancy, she and David have become the parents of Luke, Helen, Jane, and Paul, all under the age of eight. Since grandmother Dorothy is now needed by her other daughters, her availability is no longer there for the asking. David, meanwhile, borrows ever-increasing sums from his father. The garden remains neglected. Such is the scene of "welcome" that greets the new baby.

None of Harriet's pregnancies has been easy, but this one, right from the start, causes her so much pain that she resorts to sedatives and tranquillizers, which she begs from her doctor and then, secretly, from her sisters. The fetus, day and night, seems to her like a ravaging monster—an enemy, a "wrestler," who batters her mercilessly from within. Concealing her suffering as best she can, she grows increasingly silent and morose. Feeling guilty and irrationally responsible because what is happening is going on inside her own body, she becomes aware of an unprecedented gap between David and herself. If she talked openly to him, he would be unsympathetic, she fears, like her male gynecologist, Dr. Brett, who refuses to credit her terrors and denies that anything out of the ordinary is going on.

Plagued by an incessant jabbing and jolting inside her womb, Harriet finds she must keep herself in perpetual motion to distract herself from the fetus, which seems to be trying to tear its way out of her body. In anguish, she takes to pacing the floor ceaselessly and even the streets. Lessing offers the most horrifying description of pregnancy I have ever read:

"She almost ran through streets she hardly saw, hour after hour, until she understood she was causing comment. Then she took to driving a short way out of town, where she walked along the country lanes, fast, sometimes running. People in passing cars would turn, amazed, to see this hurrying driven woman, white-faced, hair flying, open-mouthed, panting, arms clenched across her front. If they stopped to offer help, she shook her head and ran on" (41).

What, all the while, is she thinking? She is imagining, of course, the child-to-be. I see her conjuring monsters, fiends, freaks, all manner of misshapen and ferocious beasts, for what is growing inside her cannot be a familiar being like the others—a tiny developing humanoid that kicks and stretches with delicate unformed hands and feet—but, instead, some hybrid brute with claws or hooves that rips, scrapes, and digs savagely at her.

Delivery, at last, brings relief. But what is revealed turns out to be an uncomely infant, yellowish, stony-eyed, oversized, and heavy, as well as preternaturally strong. Stiff, unable to relax in her arms, the newborn clamps down and bites her with his gums. Just as when he was inside her, he attacks. He does not seem "like a baby at all," Harriet thinks, and her immediate reaction, after being released from the agony of pregnancy, is to pity him—the "poor little beast," as she silently calls him. Ironically, perhaps wistfully, she names him Ben, the Hebrew word for "son."

I want to linger here. For, in these scenes, Lessing conjures up a transgressive image of childbirth that may send us back, by contrast, to the grace and loveliness of the *Madonna del Parto* mentioned earlier in these pages and to other serene Madonnas painted with their babies in their arms. Is there, after all, any event in human life for which we are more primed to derive joy than the arrival of a newborn child?

Even in families in which want and privation are rife, the welcoming of an infant often calls forth joy and, not infrequently, a lavish expenditure of scant resources so as to provide auspicious rites and ceremonies (see Mead 1960). Many non-Christians, as well as Christians, for example, take pleasure during the winter holiday season in hearing and even singing the traditional European carols and recalling the tender imagery that heralds—both musically and visually—the birth of a child that not all claim as their savior. Why? Perhaps because, with the beginning of new life come promises of renewal and hope. Perhaps because, whoever we are, we seem to subscribe to the unqualified goodness and sweetness of a newborn infant and to the notion of opportunity that his or her birth holds out—however fleetingly—for betterment and progress. One more chance to get things right. This time around. With each newborn child comes the possibility of future salvation and a better world.

I recall a studious young man in my own family who telephoned his faraway mother from a lying-in hospital in New England just after his baby's birth, and, in a voice breaking with emotion, managed to tell her that, although he had experienced moments of intense joy, he had never until then shed tears of happiness. (Unbeknownst to him, his own mother had, when he was born, similarly wept.) In fact, on that latter occasion, an attending nurse had wondered aloud, rather crudely, why the new mother was crying now that her labor pains were over. This nurse was quickly admonished by an older and wiser aide, who enlightened her by explaining that *these* were tears of gratitude and exultation.

An instance of this supreme valuation of new life has been recited in my presence annually, a holy day prayer that never fails to chasten me:

"If some messenger were to come to us with the offer that death should be overthrown, but with the one inseparable condition that birth should also cease; if the existing generation were given the chance to live for ever, but on the clear understanding that never again would there be a child, . . . could the answer be in doubt?" (Stern 1984).

Such a passage rings with the reverence we accord new human life; it reminds us that, while it is undeniably founded on the biological imperative to reproduce and preserve our species, that imperative comes to us overlaid with intricate brocades of cultural elaboration.

Suppose, however, that an event could subvert that joy and make a mockery of it. An event that made us question whether childbirth is indeed a summum bonum and whether children are indeed blessed from the start. Suppose an infant, eagerly awaited by family and friends, proved monstrous. All attempts to love and understand him failed. He remained hostile and unrelated. What then?

As an artist, Lessing seeks to explore this eventuality, and this is what she conjures. Her other characters cannot attach themselves to the inscrutable Ben nor he to them. Lost in a warren of hopeless practical and moral dilemmas, the Lovatt family descends—after Ben's birth—into strife and plummets into fragmentation. Despite attempts to integrate him into the existing fabric of the family while preserving the others intact and protecting them from his unpredictable spates of escalating violence (presently to be described), they fail. Eventually the older children's rooms must be locked at night against him. A miasma of terror, distrust, guilt, and recrimination spreads. The family's close-knit tissue shreds.

When Lessing introduces Ben, the reader feels, almost instinctively, a need to understand him and explain his demonic presence, for his violence, palpable in the womb, merely increases with age. At barely eighteen months, he unaccountably strangles a terrier and, to the family's horror, kills the poor animal. Three months later, using his hands in the same way for the same purpose (he is still under two years of age), he smothers and kills the family's beloved cat, Mr. McGregor, who had feared him from the start and tried in vain to keep out of his way. At three, Ben attempts to take the life of another pet, and at five he startles and disgusts the family by grabbing a raw chicken from the refrigerator and savagely dismembering it with his teeth and fingers while snarling over its spilled carcass. He attempts to attack, perhaps even kill, his cousin Amy, who is afflicted with Down syndrome, and he badly injures his brother Paul by nearly breaking his arm. Murder is, of course, unknown to a child of this age, but the violence that motivates each of these acts cannot be gainsaid. Whence such fiendishness?

Determined to salvage something of their former life, the family decides (against Harriet's wishes) to banish Ben, before he is four years old, to an institution in the north of England where, notwithstanding euphemistic descriptions to the contrary, freakish children are trussed, drugged, and eventually destroyed by increasing doses of sedation. Harriet is racked with remorse and plagued by fantasies of her child's incarceration. Against the combined will and advice of the rest of her family, she who bore him and gave him birth travels secretly to the north, finds him, and brings him home. In so doing, she saves his life, for she finds him straightjacketed, smeared with excrement, and drugged into temporary oblivion. She saves his life, however, at the cost of her other children, who now, because of the danger he once again presents, must be sent away to boarding schools and relatives' homes for safety, and also at the cost of her marriage, for her husband abandons her emotionally in disgust. At the end of the story, even Ben himself, who has never been able to connect with her or show her any recognition or affection, departs, and she is left entirely alone. Having failed to protect either the one child or herself or the rest of her family, Harriet sits by herself in front of the television set wondering what would have happened if she had let him die—which she could not do—and what will become of him out in the world and whether she saved him for an even worse fate.

Thus, shockingly, Lessing destabilizes our rosy myths about the unmitigated glory of childbirth. She blasts the supposed joys of parenthood. Pinning us against an abrasive wall, she makes us flinch under her fierce authorial gaze. What does it mean—she asks us—to become and to *be* a parent (they are not the same)? Why do people want to have children, and how dare we assume that terrible risk? She moves us to realize that, even in cases in which becoming a parent is carefully considered, people tend to bypass the fundamental question as to *why* a child is wanted. Debates over reproductive rights and personal freedoms likewise neglect the question, for our default assumption is that birth and parenthood are unquestionably desirable.

Today, of course, voices rise in dissent, voices that emphasize global issues—population explosion, scarcity of resources, environmental sustainability, health, education, women's rights to freedom from biological determinism, and so on. Yet even protesters on these grounds retain, as a default position, the notion that having babies is good—a good that simply needs to be monitored and controlled.

The Fifth Child charges us to reexamine that position. Powerful when it first appeared in the late 1980s, Lessing's horror tale has gained in relevance with the passing years. Today, while a small percentage of human life on the planet is being prolonged to unprecedented lengths by miracles of modern medicine, sanitation, and nutrition, a vastly larger percentage is being mindlessly created without regard for its future welfare or even survival, and no longer can there be any cogent argument for the *need* to produce a biological heir.

And who, after all, *is* this alien child character Ben? What are the reasons for his existence? After all, aren't all children benign or at least neutral from the start? Is it the child himself who shatters his family or is it the dreams and delusions, the self-deceptions and false steps taken by others before his birth as well as afterward, that are at fault? Who, if anyone, is to blame? Lessing wants us to notice how images formed in advance of children's arrival cast far-reaching shadows and how mothers and fathers often have different perspectives. (David cannot forgive Harriet for bringing Ben back from the institution.) Ethical choices and parenting decisions overlap but do not always match.

The story's deepest horror—as I have indicated—springs, in my view, from its challenge to what is evoked by Piero's beautiful Madonna, its brazen undermining of the ethos of that painting. Furthermore, Ben's traumatic birth, his recalcitrant unintelligibility, and his hostile recidivism open, by implication, an inquiry into the role of chance, fate, and evil in human life. Because Ben is the antithesis of a sweet baby, he fails to inspire love. Instead, he evokes pity and fear, the very emotions Aristotle names in his *Poetics* as fundamental to tragedy. Lessing succeeds in assuring, moreover, that Ben exists not only as a fictional entity—that is, between the covers of her book—but also in our minds as we read. She plants him in us, just as she plants him in Harriet, so that, once we have encountered him, he cannot be willed away. Lessing herself, after the book came out, spoke to a *New York Times* reviewer as follows:

"I hated writing it . . . It was sweating blood. I was very glad when it was done. It was an upsetting thing to write—obviously, it goes very deep into me somewhere" (quoted in Rothstein 1988).

Ben's subjectivity, moreover, remains opaque. We encounter him solely through the eyes of the narrator and other characters. Whereas other works discussed in these pages engage us with children's perceptions as imagined by writers and auteurs, here, from cover to cover, Ben comes to us from perspectives located outside rather than inside his own head. We watch him. We learn what he looks like and how he behaves, what he finally speaks (his first words, when he is two and a half, are "I want cake"), but never do we find out how he feels or what he thinks or believes. Lessing does not take us inside. Anything we surmise about his inner life comes from our own projections and fantasies.

What is the effect of this narrative choice? For many readers, it works to alienate Ben just as he is alienated from the members of his own family. This is because, when Lessing backs away from giving him an inner voice, we sense that he is so barbaric even she cannot imagine what motivates him. Her decision to avoid his mental world not only places us radically outside it but challenges us to ask whether it exists at all and then to wonder by implication whether this character can rightly be considered human since to be human is to be endowed with mind. Terms used for Ben by other characters include *changeling, goblin,* and *throwback.*

In other stories where human characters give birth to apparently nonhuman ones, this is not always the case. *Stuart Little,* by E. B. White (1945), takes us straight into the mind and heart of its title character, a charming mouse born to an ordinary New York City matron, and we are encouraged to sympathize with him. Such retention of recognizable human qualities by apparently nonhuman characters is a feature of many well-known texts in the literary canon, including, notably, the ancient *Golden Ass* of Apuleius, the fairy tale of *Beauty and the Beast* in its multiple variants, Kafka's *Metamorphosis* (1915), *The Elephant Man* (Pomerance 1979), *E.T. the Extra-Terrestrial* (Spielberg 1982), and *Shrek!* (Steig 1990), among countless others. What Lessing concocts is different. She presents a monstrous body that houses an unfathomable mind. Only with such a double-barreled weapon, as it were, can she get us to reassess our cherished beliefs.

Sometimes, when I teach *The Fifth Child,* my tenderhearted undergraduate students balk and try their best to infuse Ben with a range of human motives. They imagine a point of view for him and attribute it to him. They come to acknowledge eventually that these readings mainly depend on projection and that, into the gaping holes of Lessing's text, they have dolloped spoonfuls of their own sensibility. Their efforts stem from deeply engaged forms of reading, however, and their desires to tame and humanize Ben often lead them to more nuanced perceptions of what actually does and does not inhere in the text and to a keener grasp of how boundaries between ourselves and the characters we meet blur in the reading process when an author's words are keenly felt.

Beyond this, and more specifically, my students come to appreciate that, by adding their own thoughts and feelings to Lessing's title character as he is written, they are in fact gentling him for their own ends. They are rendering him at least minimally intelligible and sympathetic. This allows them to evade the frightful anxiety that would ensue from their *not* understanding him, from fearing what he might do next. It prevents them from feeling helpless, along with the other characters in the story, just as Ben himself feels helpless with regard to himself and to the world. To project their sensibility into Ben is to flee the terror he generates and to be liberated, to some extent, from the plight of his family. It is to preserve a measure of their own preexistent comfort zone. Achieving a kind of mastery permits them to bypass Lessing's claim that she has written a "classic horror story" (quoted in Rothstein 1988). Toning Ben down, turning him into a victim, calling him a maligned outsider or a misunderstood child, diagnosing or pathologizing him in psychiatric terms, as autistic, say, or explaining him as a symbol of the moral failures of his parents or society in general makes reading the book a lot easier and, as Lessing would scornfully say, "safe."

Let's return now to a time before the advent of Ben, when Harriet and David are newly married, for much is revealed then that can be seen as predictive—though not causative—of what is to come. The couple's first child, a boy called Luke, is conceived the very day they take possession of their oversized exurban house.

Parenthetically, we may note, from the surname Lovatt, Lessing's conceit of toying slyly with names, and, in a novel devoted to the bearing and rearing of children, the name Luke might well invoke the third Gospel writer who, indeed, gives us our fullest account of Mary's pregnancy and the nativity of Jesus. It is the Gospel according to Luke and no other that offers the spoken voice of Mary, and, consulting the history of art, we note, too, that it is the apostle Luke who, portrayed as an artist, untiringly draws pictures of the Virgin and Child. Ironically, Ben, the sole Lovatt child who cannot express love, receives the name meaning *son*. Surely, as suggested earlier, this should be read as hopeful as well as sardonic—as a quasi-magical wish fulfillment on Harriet's part. She, a beleaguered mother who has just endured a pregnancy from hell, bestows it wistfully on this most unfilial of infants. At the same time, whereas the other children, who can and do love her, have, as it were, "Christian" names, this one, the so-called throwback, is given a Hebraic one.

Both Lovatts at this point have jobs in London, and their plan after the wedding is to continue commuting from the outlying area where their house is situated so as to earn enough money to start a family. That plan has no chance. The day they acquire the house, they walk hand in hand through its empty rooms, populating them in fantasy with hordes of romping children, and then, although they have brought along no contraceptive devices, find themselves making love not once or twice but, Lessing emphasizes, three times.

Knowing she is within the fertile days of her menstrual cycle, Harriet lies there on a bed left by previous owners and experiences a pang of sudden fear. David, however, brazenly laughs. It is "a loud, reckless, unscrupulous laugh," as Lessing describes it, "quite unlike [the] modest, humorous, judicious David" we know. Chilled, Harriet fails to recognize him. He grips her arm tightly to silence any incipient protest. Later, after they have dressed and are returning by car to London in the rain, she asks how they will manage if she is pregnant. Only then does David awaken to the fact that, despite whatever humiliation it might cause him, he will have to beg money from his wealthy father.

Thus, in a moment of sexual abandon, Harriet and David, who come together on the basis of a mutual revulsion from what they perceive as the sexual irresponsibility of others, initiate a fateful cycle of excess and dependency of their own. In Lessing's framing of the scene, there is a split second when "Harriet almost cried out, 'No, stop! What are you doing?'" But she yields to David's need to make the future happen. Without overreading, I think we can sense here a certain demonic element, at least an innuendo, especially because David turns momentarily alien and feels like a stranger to Harriet (and to us).

Harriet and David's first baby, Luke, however, proves a contented child with pink cheeks and eyes of blue; yet an undercurrent of malignancy swells page by page until, with the birth of Ben, it overwhelms the couple's marriage and demolishes their "idyll." Harriet, while still virginal and resisting the mores of her time, had styled herself a "misfit." This very term *misfit* resurfaces later in the novel and becomes an epithet for Ben. We should not gloss over this coincidence, for it connects the two with a tragic bond of identification, especially when we learn that, even though it means sacrificing everything else in her life, Harriet cannot give Ben up.

We may not, however, conclude that Lessing means merely to indict Harriet (and David) for hypocrisy or to explain their fifth child away as a kind of demonic retribution. What she reveals rather is a deep psychological truth, namely, that an unexamined revulsion often leads to a displaced reenactment of what has been reviled. Thus, the irresponsible sexuality Harriet and David once found so loathsome in others recurs within their own marriage. We tend, moreover, to resist the idea that an "evil" like Ben simply occurs, but, as the philosopher Susan Neiman (2002) points out, we seek rational explanations because they seem to put us back in charge, and we are more at home with agency than with notions of fate or chance. In *The Fifth Child*, such unpalatable ideas, I am convinced, are exactly what Lessing wants us to entertain.

Granted the extreme valuation of pregnancy and giving birth, perhaps it would help to project and imagine a scene in which we participate vicariously. You are a new mother who has just emerged from anesthesia or simply raised your head after the ordeal of delivery and are handed your baby. Instead of the soft little human being you expect, you discover you have produced a monster. You are shown a creature who does not resemble you and seems frightening because of its strangeness. Yet, this living being has just come out of *your* body. Has been a part of you, has cohabited with you, has lived inside of you for nine long months, has been nourished internally by you, is, in fact, *your child*. How do you feel?

Before answering, I would like to return for a moment to the notion of "defamiliarization" and use it here in our imaginary scene, which is, of course, merely a variation on Lessing's portrayal of Harriet's first moments with Ben. Could we, with this tool, actually read this highly disturbing scene as connected with lived experience? Could we read it, in fact, as a recognizable account of any mother's initial experience of giving birth? For, after all, the wizened newborn is always strange. No parent is prepared for what will emerge from the womb; thus, an element of surprise always lurks in the moment of birth. Those who are present may experience a shiver at the first sight of that tiny being who was invisible for so long and yet so unmistakably present.

In my family, we children were regularly regaled with a story meant to amuse us but which actually disquieted me. A distinguished legal scholar-uncle was taken, as a small boy, to view a newborn cousin and blurted out in a lisp to the frail new mother, "Aunt Wothe [Rose], that baby lookth juth like a monkey!" A reaction which may remind some readers of a child's unforgettable cry when a gullible monarch marches stark naked in Hans Christian Andersen's cunning tale *The Emperor's New Clothes*. Like these two uninhibited children, Lessing yanks off the distorting lenses of our idealizations and deceptions. She makes us see how an artist, like a child—albeit speaking from a different platform—brazenly utters truths we obscure behind velvet mantles woven of words.

My point is not that all babies are monsters, nor am I suggesting that by evoking the notion of defamiliarization we can account for Ben and wish away his disturbing strangeness. Rather, it is that the critical tool of defamiliarization may help us connect Harriet's experience with our own by reading art—even at its most outré—as intimately connected with our ordinary lives and as redolent of points about our lives that we tend to disavow.

Ben, for example, is called many names throughout Lessing's book. He is referred to, from time to time, not only as a monster but as a *beast*, a *leech*, a *troll*, an *enemy*, an *alien*, a *savage*, a *Neanderthal*, a *hobgoblin*, a *gnome*, and a *destroyer*, among other pejoratives. These epithets spell the gap that exists between what his parents had expected and what he turns out to be; they increase the gap to several powers. Some of us may recoil and feel offended by them. We may balk at the application of such immoderate terms to an infant and later on to a child. Because of them, we build up a mental picture of Ben that matches them even though we do so with inner turmoil, piously telling ourselves that *we* ourselves would never so describe our own children or other children we know.

Yet how honest is that sentiment? A sheepish inner tug warns that, when we are truthful, we can well recall moments when even the most lovable of children has seemed monstrous and alien, rebellious and destructive. Such moments fly past. They are rarely acted on or spoken of aloud or even admitted into full consciousness. We protect our offspring and ourselves from ungentle thoughts. Lessing asks us to face them here and own them, for they are an authentic element in our lives just as they are in the highly exaggerated world of her novel.

By living out in genuine discomfort (the discomfort matters) extremes we cannot allow ourselves consciously to undergo in life, we may be able to cultivate a greater range of sensitivity and openness to experience—our own as well as that of others. In a book devoted to the reading of art for life, this should be our goal. Defamiliarization provides lenses that—when we put them on—empower us to stare a little more bravely at Lessing's uncanny world and, for better or worse, recognize ourselves in it rather than rejecting it outright. Fitfully blending the queasy with the cozy, Lessing constructs her art out of what we already know but do not want to know. And, incidentally, she wrote the book twice; she threw away her first draft because it struck her as too "soft" and hence as insufficiently authentic.

Pregnant women often daydream, and sometimes they have nightmares about giving birth to a child who is abnormal in some way, defective, or freakish. These fears are quickly suppressed and rarely recalled in years to come. They are not confined to mothers-to-be but afflict fathers-to-be and likewise children who are about to acquire a new brother or sister. Can you recall any trepidation of your own of a similar kind? Surely, we would be correct to classify them under "dread of the unknown" for, in the vacuum caused by waiting—and nine months is, after all, a long time to anticipate a momentous event over which we have little control—fantasies proliferate, like mold in dank crevices. A particularly vivid and graphic example of prenatal fantasy was reported to me by a psychologist whose pregnant wife awakened him one night with a scream after dreaming that, when she opened the oven door, an enormous rat leaped out.

Such fears include notions that the baby may turn out to be scaly-skinned and serpentine or a "parasitic invader" of the uterus or a "tiny, ugly, helpless, rubbery, disconnected" thing (see Raphael-Leff 1993) or that it may resemble some monstrous hybrid, as in notions of minotaurs, satyrs, and sphinxes. Works of art, moreover, draw on such fears. Mary Shelley's *Frankenstein* springs to mind, a book that links on many levels with pregnancy (see Waites 1991; and Almond 1998). Shelley's own mother died just days after giving birth to her. Later on, before Mary herself—at barely seventeen—eloped with the married poet Percy Bysshe Shelley, she and Shelley were holding secret trysts in her mother's graveyard. Merely seven months after the elopement, Mary delivered a premature baby girl who died in less than two weeks and then, scarcely two years later, while writing *Frankenstein,* she lost yet another child and was again pregnant with her third by the poet. Thus, the monster in her story condenses a staggering complex of losses, fears, and mergers of birth with death as well as terrors thereof.

We can locate such fantasies about monstrous children in other works as well, such as Henry James's *Turn of the Screw* (1898), where the governess suspects her young charges Miles and Flora of having been demonized by their former caretakers in unspeakable ways redolent of sexual innuendo. A spate, moreover, of mid- to late-twentieth-century movies portrays child characters who often prove bestial and evil: *The Bad Seed* (1956), *The Innocents* (1961), *Rosemary's Baby* (1968), *The Exorcist* (1973), *The Omen* (1976), *Demon Seed* (1977), *Children of the Corn* (1984), and others, all of which depict children in wicked, strange, and/or disturbing roles.

Counterphobically, mothers check their newborn infants in the hospital; nervous with anxiety, they count fingers and toes and scan the often blotchy skin for permanently disfiguring marks. What young child, furthermore, watching his or her mother's belly swell, has not wondered what sort of creature might be growing inside her and what it will be like when it comes out?

Apropos of such fantasies and fears on the part of children, the distinguished New York psychologist, the late Dr. Martha Wolfenstein, conducted pioneering research that was published postwar in 1947. Wolfenstein commissioned a prominent writer of her time, Leo Rosten, to create a story that would capture children's fantasies and anxieties about what might be growing inside a pregnant mother. Gathering pairs of mothers and children, Wolfenstein asked the former to read Rosten's story aloud to their offspring. Her hypothesis was that the story might serve as a projective device allowing both parents and children to release hidden feelings about the birth of a new baby. She surmised that the story would prove useful and serve as a catharsis for traumatic worries or, alternatively, that it might induce and exacerbate them. Of special interest is that the protagonist of Rosten's story, a little girl named Sally, after being told about the new baby, does not of course know precisely when it will appear or what gender it will be. Consequently, Sally decides that when she grows up she will arrange things more carefully and give birth to exactly the offspring she wants: part bunny, part kitty, and part duck. She calls this creature a Rampatan and then wonders how it would be if her mother actually gave birth to a Rampatan instead of a baby.

Wolfenstein analyzes Rosten's story and details the reactions of her experimental subjects. Thus, she shows us how an artwork can be tapped for insights into human feelings and how Lessing's later character, Ben, is a participant in a long continuum of imaginative creations that emanate from our ongoing fascination with the mysterious origins of human life.

Lessing, as I have tried to show, weaves her fearsome tale with skill and craft. Like Gretel, she strews the path with clues for us to gather so as to make and unmake our way and to forge and then doubt our explanations. When all is said and done, however, the clues do not add up (to Ben), and we, like the characters within the novel, cannot account for him. Nor can we account with surety for the temperaments, the evolving personalities, or the surprising fates of our own children. Monstrous and unresponsive as they, too, may seem at times, and as we in turn seem, no doubt, to them, we love them. We are loathe to abandon them. Even if they, like Ben, should ever abandon us.

I see Lessing's work as a wrenching call for the strength to withstand uncertainty and not only in art. Life, where deeds are required, also rewards tolerance for ambiguity. Harriet saved Ben, her alien child, and sacrificed all the others in so doing. She was unable to act otherwise. To ask whether she was right or wrong crushes her into the binary model we know but must refuse. Dwelling in her story as Lessing tells it is to experience oneself as humbly implicated in some of parenthood's most intractable riddles. It means realizing that to ask and ponder is more valuable than settling on any fixed answer. Hedged round with doubt, we turn the pages, absorbing, as we read, a measure of art's wisdom.

An Interactive Afterword

The gifted writers, filmmakers, and artists whose works we have been living with in these pages have swept us along on wings of fantasy, wafted us with conjuring wands through moving panoramas, into alien dreams, onto stages set with props and furniture we may not have seen before, and out of ordinary time. They have shown us extremes of attitude and conduct that, with the prompt of defamiliarization, have seemed, perhaps, less outré than otherwise and more readily assimilable. Why not go back now and revisit these realms? Reread the books. Watch the films. Adopt a child like Ben or Ludo. Reconceive yourself as Diana or Harriet or Walter Lee or as one of the several grandparents. What about the children? Could you be Annie, Molly, Mendel, Travis, Momik, or Ponette? Could you be Ben? I invite you to re-experience these works and to reinvent them in your own terms—and then to return home psychically.

At the end of the semester, I ask my undergraduate students to select a few of their favorite characters from the plays, novels, and short stories we have read together and from the films we have watched. I ask them to bring these characters back to life in any century, at any time of year, or day, or in any geographic location they like with total freedom to opt for out-of-time or other wildly fantastic scenarios. Where will your characters meet, I ask? What will they talk about? How will they relate to one another? What will they agree or disagree about?

Compose a dialogue for them; make it a minidrama or a farce, if you prefer. Be as inventive, adventurous, or zany as you dare. But stay with your characters and get to know each one as deeply as you can.

My students enjoy this assignment because it gives them a chance to range back freely over all we have shared together and to exercise their wondrous, underutilized imaginations. The results are surprising, clever, insightful, sometimes hilarious, and occasionally deeply moving. On an airplane once, my seatmate, a stranger, asked me if I were ill because I was apparently sniffling, but I replied, "Not at all." I had been responding to one of my students' end-of-term dialogues. In it the young man had rewritten a portion of the *Odyssey* so as to have Telemachus actually find Odysseus and save his life, a plot twist that stunningly intuits the very deepest unspoken wish this bereft youth must have cherished as he searched the seas for his missing father.

In this spirit, I encourage you, dear reader, to range back over the preceding chapters and the works to which they refer. Not, perhaps, with the aim of creating a dialogue (although, why not?) but for that "second moment" of aesthetic experience, as philosopher Arnold Isenberg once put it, and with the idea of noticing themes that have recurred. Conflicts, say, between a child's wishes and the constraints of his or her social milieu, the parents caught squirming. Or the problems of history—the parents' longer sense of it versus their children's wishes to escape it altogether or to ferret out aspects of it that the parents wish to hide. Or the theme of stubborn rootedness to one's ground instead of ranging, questing, and taking in ever wider fields of vision and comprehension. What about missed opportunities for compromise, for listening and reflection? Binary straightjackets. Reciprocal mendacity and wished-for truth telling on the part of children and parents alike. Secrecy's unsuspected cross-generational collusions. Pertinacious loyalty, ingenuity, and passion. The refusal, nearly ubiquitous, to give up. These are just a few.

As Nadine Gordimer (1991) writes in her introduction to the prose of Joseph Roth, the bond between parent and child is "perhaps the most mysterious and fateful of all human relationships, the [one] whose influence runs beneath and often outlasts those between sexual partners. We are children and we are parents: there is no dissolution of these states except death."

What will it be like afterward, for you? Will you go back to those you love and care for with your ears more finely tuned and your eyes more keenly focused? Or will all the magic dissipate in stark daylight? As golden Pam seems mischievously to imply, when she winks knowingly at us and flies languorously past on that silver screen, trailing stardust. . . .

I wonder.

References

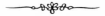

Aeschylus I. 1953. Oresteia. In *The Complete Greek Tragedies*. Tr. Richmond Lattimore. Chicago: University of Chicago Press.

Almond, Barbara R. 1998. The Monster Within: Mary Shelley's Frankenstein and a Patient's Fears of Childbirth and Mothering. *International Journal of Psycho-Analysis* 79:775–86.

Barzun, Jacques. 1944. *Teacher in America*. Indianapolis: Liberty Fund.

Berliner, Alain. 1997. *Ma vie en rose*. Haut et court. Sony Pictures Classics. Film in French, English subtitles.

Bettelheim, Bruno. 1950. *Love Is Not Enough*. New York: Avon Books.

Bettelheim, Bruno. 1976. *The Uses of Enchantment*. New York: Knopf.

Breuer, Josef, and Sigmund Freud. [1895] 1953. Case Histories. Case 1: Fraulein Anna O (Breuer). In "Studies on Hysteria." *The Standard Edition of the Complete Psychological Works of Sigmund Freud*. Tr. and ed. James Strackey, vol. 2, 21–47. London: Hogarth Press.

Bruner, Jerome. [1960] 2003. *The Process of Education*. Cambridge: Harvard University Press.

Buber, Martin, 1958. *I and Thou*. 2nd ed. Tr. Ronald Gregor Smith. New York: Charles Scribner's Sons.

Célan, Paul. [1947] 2002. Todesfuge. In *Poems of Paul Célan*. Tr. Michael Hamburger. New York: Persea Books.

Cranshaw, Edward. 1969. *Maria Theresa*. London: Sphere Books.

Damisch, Hubert. 2007. *A Childhood Memory by Piero della Francesca*. Tr. John Goodman. Palo Alto: Stanford University Press.

Doillon, Jacques. 1996. *Ponette*. Film starring Victoire Thivisol. Les Films Alain Sarde Rhone-Alpes Cinéma; DVD format with English subtitles. Fox Lorber FLV 1371 VHS.

Dutton, Denis. 2009. *The Art Instinct: Beauty, Pleasure, and Human Evolution*. New York: Bloomsbury.

Erikson, Erik H. 1968. *Identity, Youth, and Crisis.* New York: Norton.

Feldman, Yael. 2008. Personal communication, May 28.

First, Ruth. 1965. *117 Days: An Account of Confinement and Interrogation under the South African Ninety-Day Detention Law.* London: Bloomsbury.

Frankel, Glenn. 1999. *Rivonia's Children: Three Families and the Price of Freedom in South Africa.* New York: Farrar, Straus, and Giroux.

Freud, Sigmund. [1905] 1953. Fragment of an Analysis of a Case of Hysteria. In *The Standard Edition of the Complete Psychological Works of Sigmund Freud.* Tr. and ed. James Strachey, vol. 7, 7–122. London: Hogarth Press.

Gallaz, Christophe, and Roberto Innocenti. 1985. *Rose Blanche.* San Diego: Harcourt, Brace.

Gaskell, Elizabeth C. [1855] 1994. *North and South.* Were, Hertfordshire: Wordsworth Editions.

Golomb, Claire. 2004. *The Child's Creation of a Pictorial World.* Mahwah, N.J.: Erlbaum.

Gopnick, Alison. 2009. *The Philosophical Baby.* New York: Farrar, Straus, and Giroux.

Gordimer, Nadine. 1979. *Burger's Daughter.* Harmondsworth: Penguin.

Gordimer, Nadine. [1991] 1995. Introduction to *The Radetzky March* by Joseph Roth. Tr. Joachim Neugroschel, vii–xx. Woodstock, N.Y.: Overlook Press.

Graham, Jorie. 1983. *Erosion.* Princeton: Princeton University Press.

Grossman, David. 1989. *See Under: LOVE.* Tr. Betsy Rosenberg. New York: Farrar, Straus, and Giroux.

Hansberry, Lorraine. 1959. *A Raisin in the Sun.* New York: Vintage Books.

Hegel, Georg Wilhelm Friedrich. [1807] 1967. *The Phenomenology of Mind.* Tr. J. B. Baillie. New York: Harper Torchbooks.

Hoban, Russell, and Lillian Hoban. 1964. *Bread and Jam for Frances.* New York: Harper and Row.

Hugo, Victor. [1930] 1950. Lorsque l'enfant parait. In *Victor Hugo: Poesies,* vol. 1. Paris: Librairie Hachette.

Hume, David. 1998. *Dialogues Concerning Natural Religion.* Oxford: Oxford University Press.

Ibsen, Henrik. [1884] 1961. *The Wild Duck.* In *Hedda Gabler and Other Plays.* Tr. Una Ellis-Fermor. London: Penguin. Originally published in Norwegian.

Isenberg, Arnold. 1973. *Aesthetics and the Theory of Criticism.* Ed. W. Callaghan et al. Chicago: University of Chicago Press.

James, Henry. [1898] 1968. *The Turn of the Screw.* In *The Turn of the Screw and Daisy Miller.* New York: Lancer Books.

James, William. [1899] 1925. *Talks to Teachers.* New York: Henry Holt.

Jones, Ernest. [1943] 1961. *The Life and Work of Sigmund Freud.* New York: Anchor Books.

Kafka, Franz. [1915] 1996. *The Metamorphosis and Other Stories.* Tr. Stanley Appelbaum. New York: Dover Publications.

Kincaid, Jamaica. 1985. *Annie John*. New York and London: Penguin Books.

Klarsfeld, Serge, ed. 1996. *French Children of the Holocaust: A Memorial*. New York: New York University Press.

Lessing, Doris. 1988. *The Fifth Child*. New York: Vintage Books.

MacGillivray, James. 2002. Andrei Tarkovsky's Madonna del Parto. *Canadian Journal of Film Studies/Revue canadienne d'études cinématographiques* 11, no. 2 (fall 2002): 82–100.

Mandela, Nelson. 1995. *Long Walk to Freedom*. Boston: Little, Brown.

Mead, Margaret. 1960. *Four Families*. National Film Board of Canada. Film.

Miller, Alice. 1981. *The Drama of the Gifted Child*. Tr. Ruth Ward. New York: Basic Books.

Neiman, Susan. 2002. *Evil in Modern Thought*. Princeton: Princeton University Press.

Nietzsche, Friedrich. 1874. *On the Use and Abuse of History for Life*. Tr. Ian Johnston. Nanaimo, B.C.: Vancouver Island University, E-text.

Paley, Vivian Gussin. 1999. *The Kindness of Children*. Cambridge, Mass., and London: Harvard University Press.

Pomerance, Bernard. 1979. *The Elephant Man*. New York: Grove Press.

Raphael-Leff, Joan. 1993. *Pregnancy: The Inside Story*. London: Sheldon Press.

Rosler, Alexander. 1997. *Mendel*. Film. Released by First Run Features.

Rothstein, Mervyn. 1988. The Painful Nurturing of Doris Lessing's "Fifth Child." *New York Times,* June 14.

Safire, William. 2008. "The Seamy Side of Semiotics." Column on Language. *International Herald Tribune,* May 26, 9.

Semel, Nava. 2008. *And the Rat Laughed*. Tr. Miriam Shlesinger. Melbourne, Australia: Hybrid Publishers.

Sendak, Maurice. 1963. *Where the Wild Things Are*. New York: Harper and Row.

Shelley, Mary Wollstonecraft. [1818, 1831] 1994. *Frankenstein*. London: Macmillan Tor Classics.

Shklovskij, Viktor. [1925] 1990. *Theory of Prose*. Tr. Benjamin Sher. Normal, Ill.: Dakley Archive Press.

Slovo, Shawn. 1988. *A World Apart*. Film. Director: Chris Menges.

Sophocles I. 1954. Oedipus the King. In *The Complete Greek Tragedies,* ed. David Grene and Richmond Lattimore, 11–76. Chicago: University of Chicago Press.

Spielberg, Stephen. 1982. *E.T. the Extra-Terrestrial*. Film.

Spitz, Ellen Handler. 1985. *Art and Psyche*. New Haven and London: Yale University Press.

Spitz, Ellen Handler. 1998. Martha Wolfenstein: Toward the Severance of Memory from Hope. *Psychoanalytic Review* 85:105–15.

Spitz, Ellen Handler. 2001. An Essay on Beauty: Two Madonnas, the Scent of Violets, and a Family of Acrobats. *Figurationen*, no. 2: 27–34.

Steig, William. 1990. *Shrek!* New York: Farrar, Straus, and Giroux.

Stern, Chaim, ed. 1984. *The Gates of Repentence.* New York: Central Conference of American Rabbis.

Tarkovsky, Andrei. 1983. *Nostalghia.* Film.

Tarkovsky, Andrei. 1991. *Time within Time: The Diaries, 1970–1986.* Tr. Kitty Hunter-Blair. London: Faber and Faber.

Tatar, Maria. 1987. *The Hard Facts of the Grimms' Fairy Tales.* Princeton: Princeton University Press.

Thomas, Marlo, and Friends. 1972. *Free to Be You and Me.* Arista. LP album.

Tucholsky, Kurt. 1983. *Lyrik buch: Gedichte und Balladen für die Herausgegeben von Fritz Pratz.* Frankfurt-am-Main: Verlag Moritz Diesterweg.

Vasari, Giorgio. [1550] 1998. *The Lives of the Artists.* Tr. Julia Conway Bondanella and Peter Bondanella. Oxford: Oxford University Press.

Waites, Elizabeth A. 1991. Mary Shelley as Frankenstein. *Psychoanalytic Review* 78:583–98.

White, E. B. 1945. *Stuart Little.* New York: Harper and Brothers.

Wieviorka, Annette. 1999. *Auschwitz expliqué à ma fille.* Paris: Editions du Seuil.

Wilder, Thornton. [1938] 2003. *Our Town: A Play in Three Acts.* New York: Harper Perennial.

Winnicott, D. W. 1953. Transitional Objects and Transitional Phenomena. *International Journal of Psycho-Analysis* 34:89–97.

Winnicott, D. W. 1956. Primary Maternal Preoccupation. In *Collected Papers: Through Paediatrics to Psycho-Analysis, 300–305.* New York: Basic Books.

Wolfenstein, Martha. 1947. The Impact of a Children's Story on Mothers and Children. In *Monographs of the Society for Research in Child Development.* Vol. 11, serial no. 42, 1946, No. 1. Washington, D.C.: National Research Council.

Wolfenstein, Martha. 1966. How Is Mourning Possible? *Psychoanalytic Study of the Child* 21:93–123.

Wolfenstein, Martha. 1969. Loss, Rage, and Repetition. *Psychoanalytic Study of the Child* 24:432–60.

Wolfenstein, Martha. 1973. The Image of the Lost Parent. *Psychoanalytic Study of the Child* 28:433–56.

Yeats, William Butler. [1928] 1960. Among School Children. In *The Collected Poems of W. B. Yeats.* New York: Macmillan.

Zolotow, Charlotte. 1972. *William's Doll.* New York: Harper Collins.

Index

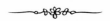